"Murray Harris . . . has provided us with a wonderful synthesis of his vast knowledge of the church at Corinth during the first century AD and how the church in the twenty-first century can apply that knowledge. He succinctly and accurately integrates historical, geographical, and archaeological information about the city and its residents. . . . The church today (laypersons, students, and pastors) will benefit from the many mature and thoughtful insights shared by Harris."

—CARL RASMUSSEN, Bethel University, emeritus

"Once again, Murray Harris delivers erudite scholarship and insight into the complex world of Corinthian Christianity in the first century. Every preacher must wrestle with the Corinthian model of church, learning as much from their mistakes as well as their example. Harris's exceptional exegesis brings to life the relationship Paul had with the church he planted, and his visits and letters written to correct and encourage their witness. Gold-star exegesis at its best."

—BRIAN N. WINSLADE, Deputy Secretary General,
    World Evangelical Alliance

"This economical treatise reaps the harvest of a lifetime of scholarly study on three continents. Harris compiles a concise summation of Paul's Corinthian letters (AD 50s) and shows how Clement of Rome addresses the same church in the AD 90s. The happy result is a crisp exposition of both Pauline letters, a glimpse into the history of the post-apostolic era, and a valuable list of application points for today. An outstanding handbook from a premier exegete and wise spiritual guide."

—ROBERT W. YARBROUGH, Covenant Theological Seminary

"Murray Harris is a master teacher. With disciplined historical imagination and profound pastoral insight, he brings the first-century Corinthian assembly to life, and from its long struggle to embody the gospel draws out lessons of urgent relevance to the twenty-first-century church. As one who had the privilege to be his student, I am delighted to see Harris's wise, learned, and engaging lectures made available to a wide audience."

—J. Ross Wagner, Duke Divinity School

"Paul's interactions with the church at Corinth provide the context for two of the most important letters of Paul. Murray Harris, who has been thinking and writing about the Corinthian correspondence for many decades, packs into this slim volume a wealth of information about the city and the early Christian letters written to the Christians there. The book provides a marvelous overview as well as appropriate points of application for today's church."

—Douglas J. Moo, Wheaton College

Renowned–But . . .

Renowned—But . . .

The Church of Corinth
in the First Century AD and its Relevance
for the Twenty-First-Century Church

MURRAY J. HARRIS

CASCADE *Books* · Eugene, Oregon

RENOWNED—BUT . . .
The Church of Corinth in the First Century AD
and Its Relevance for the Twenty-First-Century Church

Cascade Books
An Imprint of Wipf and Stock Publishers
199 W. 8th Ave., Suite 3
Eugene, OR 97401

www.wipfandstock.com

PAPERBACK ISBN: 978-1-6667-3103-3
HARDCOVER ISBN: 978-1-6667-2311-3
EBOOK ISBN: 978-1-6667-2312-0

Cataloguing-in-Publication data:

Names: Harris, Murray J., author.

Title: Renowned—but . . . : the church of Corinth in the first century AD
and its relevance for the twenty-first-century church / Murray J. Harris.

Description: Eugene, OR: Cascade Books, 2022 | Includes bibliographical
references.

Identifiers: ISBN 978-1-6667-3103-3 (paperback) | ISBN 978-1-6667-2311-3
(hardcover) | ISBN 978-1-6667-2312-0 (ebook)

Subjects: LCSH: Corinth (Greece)—History. | Bible. Corinthians—Criti-
cism, interpretation, etc. | Bible. Acts—Criticism, interpretation, etc. |
Clement I, Pope. First epistle of Clement to the Corinthians.

Classification: BS2675.2 H377 2022 (print) | BS2675.2 (ebook)

To the many students around the world,
from Norway to New Zealand,
in church or in seminary,
who have patiently heard me speak with enthusiasm
about Corinth and the Corinthian correspondence

and to

Donald A. Hagner

and

Michael W. Holmes

who both have contributed major works on First Clement

Contents

Illustrations xiii
Preface xv
Acknowledgments xvii
Abbreviations xviii
Select Bibliography xix

PART ONE: *Background*

I. The City of Corinth 1

A. History 1
    1. 146 BC: Destruction
    2. 44 BC: Restoration
    3. 27 BC: Recognition

B. Geography 4

C. Archaeology 6
    1. The Gallio Inscription
    2. The Erastus Inscription
    3. The Synagogue Inscription
    4. The *Bema*
    5. The *Diolkos*
    6. The Isthmian Games

D. Corinthian Society and the Infant Corinthian Church 14
   1. Tolerance of plurality
   2. Patent inequality
   3. Craze for adulation
   4. Pursuit of wealth
   5. Preoccupation with personal physical pleasure

PART TWO: *The Apostle Paul and Corinth*

I. Paul's Three Visits to Corinth 21

A. The Founding Visit (Acts 18:1–18) 21
   1. Aquila and Priscilla
   2. "Jesus is the Messiah"
   3. Jewish opposition

B. The "Painful (or Intermediate) Visit" 25
   1. Its historicity
   2. Its time
   3. Its occasion, purpose, and outcome

C. The Final Visit (Acts 20:2–3) 26

II. Paul's Four Letters to Corinth 28

A. The "Previous Letter" (1 Cor 5:9–10) 28
B. 1 Corinthians (see VI below) 28
C. The "Severe Letter" (2 Cor 2:3–4) 28
   1. Its purpose
   2. Its effect
   3. Its identification
D. 2 Corinthians (see VII below) 30

III. Chart Showing the Relationship of the Visits and Letters 31

IV. Chronology of the Relationship of Paul,
Timothy, and Titus with the Corinthian Church 33

V. 1 Corinthians 36

A. Occasion, Purpose, and Outcome 36
B. Basic Outlines 38
C. Outline of Content by Paragraph 38

VI. 2 Corinthians 61

A. Its Occasion, Purpose, and Outcome 61
B. Basic Outlines 62
C. Outline of Content by Paragraph 63

PART THREE: *The First Epistle of Clement
of Rome to the Corinthians*

I. Introduction 87
II. Authorship 87
III. Date **88**
IV. Text 89
V. Purpose and Content (1 Clem 54.2) 89
    A. The letter reads as a potent exhortation
    B. The letter was addressed to the whole Corinthian church
    C. The root cause of the disunity at Corinth
    D. A clarion call for harmony to replace schism at Corinth

PART FOUR: *Lessons for the Twenty-First-Century Church*

I. Features of the Corinthian church worthy of perpetual
    imitation 97
II. Potential schism as a perennial problem 98
III. Recognising the cunning tactics of the devil 99
IV. Dealing with interpersonal conflict 100
V. Accommodating vocal young people 102
VI. Encouraging submission to leadership 103
VII. Church interdependence 104
VIII. Instruction about Christian stewardship 106
IX. Exercising church discipline 111
X. Pastoral Adaptability 112

Illustrations

1. The temple of Octavia 4

2. The Corinthian theater 5

3. Map of southern Greece 6

4. The Corinth canal 7

5. The temple of Apollo and the Acrocorinth 8

6. The Gallio inscription 9

7. The Erastus inscription 11

8. The Synagogue inscription 12

9. The Bema in the Forum 13

10. The Diolkos 14

11. The Lechaion Road 16

12. The Babbius inscription 19

13. The Lower Peirene Fountain 21

Preface

My fascination with the church of Corinth began in 1965 when I began preparing for an MA exam on the Greek text of (Matthew and) 2 Corinthians. At the same time I began research on a passage in this letter (2 Cor 5:1–10) that ultimately became my (1970) doctoral dissertation. Then in 1977 I was invited to write a commentary on this letter for *The New International Greek Testament Commentary* series which finally appeared (some 28 years and 1,110 pages later!) in 2005. Also, one of my students at Trinity Evangelical Divinity School, Melissa M. Bostrom, completed her MA thesis on First Clement, and another, Michael W. Holmes, in 1989 edited and revised the standard Lightfoot–Harmer text and translation of First Clement and other works in *The Apostolic Fathers* (Grand Rapids: Baker).

A first-hand acquaintance with ancient Corinth occurred in 1973 when I spent two exciting days walking among the ruins of this city. Later, it was only standing obligations that prevented my taking up an offer from the mayor of Corinth to attend an international colloquium in 1985 on first-century Corinth.

The most authoritative and suitably illustrated guides to ancient Corinth are Nicos Papahatzis, *Ancient Corinth: The Museums of Corinth, Isthmia and Sicyon* (Athens: Ekdotike Athenon S. A., 1981); and the seventh edition site guide *Ancient Corinth: A Guide to the Site and Museum* (Princeton, NJ: American School of Classical Studies at Athens, 2018) by Guy D. R. Sanders et al. See also John McRay, *Archaeology and the New Testament* (Grand Rapids: Baker, 1991) 31–38; and David A. deSilva, "The Social and Geographical World of Roman Corinth" in the *Lexham Geographic*

Commentary on Acts through Revelation (Bellingham, WA: Lexham, 2019, ed. Barry J. Beitzel) 464–82.

The provocative title for the book was prompted by the first two chapters of First Clement where, alongside an effusive listing of all the admirable qualities that gave the church of Corinth its renowned reputation, we find an ominous reference to "the disgusting and unholy schism" (1 Clem 1:1).

It is important to observe that the "Outline of Content" that appears in Part Two in relation to 1 Corinthians (section VI) and 2 Corinthians (section VII) does not simply summarize content but also reflects exegetical decisions reached on controversial points.

All translations of ancient texts are my own.

Acknowledgments

With the kind permission of the publishers, I have made use of material, usually with changes, found in my commentaries on 2 Corinthians: in *The Expositor's Bible Commentary: Romans to Galatians* (Grand Rapids: Zondervan, 1976 and 2008); and *The Second Epistle to the Corinthians: A Commentary on the Greek Text*, The New International Greek Testament Commentary (Grand Rapids: Eerdmans, 2005).

Warm gratitude is due to Dr. Carl Rasmussen for permission to use some of his splendid photos of Corinth found at http://www.HolyLandPhotos.org.

I am grateful to two friends, Dr. Graham D. Smith and David Burt, who provided valuable comments on Part 4.

Also, I gratefully acknowledge the skillful and patient editorial work at Cascade Books of Dr. Chris Spinks, Stephanie Hough, and Heather Carraher.

Abbreviations

BDF	F. Blass, A. Debrunner, and R. W. Funk, *A Greek Grammar of the New Testament* (Chicago: University of Chicago, 1961)
Cassirer	H. W. Cassirer, *God's New Covenant: A New Testament Translation* (1989)
cf.	*confer* (Latin), compare
ESV	English Standard Version (2001)
EVV	English versions of the Bible
HCSB	Holman Christian Standard Bible (2003)
KJV	King James Version (= "Authorised Version") (1611)
LXX	Septuagint (Greek version of the OT)
NAB	New American Bible: Revised New Testament (1986)
NASB	New American Standard Bible (1977)
NIV	New International Version (2011)
NLT	New Living Translation (2013)
NRSV	New Revised Standard Version (1989)
NT	New Testament
OT	Old Testament
TCNT	Twentieth Century New Testament (1904)

Select Bibliography

(for the Corinthian correspondence and First Clement)

Barrett, C. K. *A Commentary on the First Epistle to the Corinthians.* 2nd ed. London: Black, 1971.

Bowe, Barbara E. *A Church in Crisis: Ecclesiology and Paraenesis in Clement of Rome.* Minneapolis: Fortress, 1988.

Bruce, F. F. *1 and 2 Corinthians.* London: Oliphants, 1971.

————. *Paul: Apostle of the Heart Set Free.* Grand Rapids: Eerdmans, 1977. UK title *Paul: Apostle of the Free Spirit.* Exeter: Paternoster, 1977.

Clarke, A. D. *Secular and Christian Leadership in Corinth.* Leiden: Brill, 1993.

Clarke, W. K. L. *The First Epistle of Clement to the Corinthians.* London: SPCK, 1937.

Dunn, James D. G. *The Theology of the Apostle Paul.* Grand Rapids: Eerdmans; Edinburgh: T. & T. Clark, 1998.

Engels, D. *Roman Corinth. An Alternative Model for the Classical City.* Chicago and London: University of Chicago Press, 1990.

Fee, Gordon D. *The First Epistle to the Corinthians* Grand Rapids: Eerdmans, 1987.

Grant, Robert M. *Paul in the Roman World: The Conflict at Corinth.* Louisville: Westminster John Knox, 2001.

Hagner, Donald A. *The Use of the Old and New Testaments in Clement of Rome.* Leiden: Brill, 1973.

Hall, D. R. *The Unity of the Corinthian Correspondence.* London; New York: T. & T. Clark International/Continuum, 2003.

Harris, Murray J. *The Second Epistle to the Corinthians: A Commentary on the Greek Text.* Grand Rapids: Eerdmans/Milton Keynes: Paternoster, 2005.

Harrison, J. R., and L. L. Welborn, eds. *The First Urban Christians 2: Roman Corinth.* Atlanta: SBL, 2016.

Holmberg, Bengt. *Paul and Power. The Structure of Authority in the Primitive Church as Reflected in the Pauline Epistles.* Philadelphia: Fortress, 1980.

Holmes, Michael W. *The Apostolic Fathers.* Translated by J. B. Lightfoot and J. R. Harmer, edited and revised by M. W. Holmes. 2nd ed. Grand Rapids: Baker, 1989.

————. *The Apostolic Fathers. Greek Texts and English Translations*. Edited and translated by M. W. Holmes after the earlier work of J. B. Lightfoot and J. R. Harmer. 3rd ed. Grand Rapids: Baker, 2007.

Horrell, David G. *The Social Ethos of the Corinthian Correspondence: Interests and Ideology from 1 Corinthians to 1 Clement*. Edinburgh: T. & T. Clark, 1996.

Horrell, David G., and E. Adams, eds. *Christianity at Corinth*. Louisville: Westminster John Knox, 2004.

Hurd, John C. *The Origin of 1 Corinthians*. London: SPCK, 1965.

Judge, Edwin A. *The Social Patterns of the Christian Groups in the First Century*. London: Tyndale 1960.

Kee, H. C. *Christian Origins in Sociological Perspective*. Philadelphia: Westminster, 1980.

Lampe, P. *From Paul to Valentinus: Christians at Rome in the First Two Centuries* Minneapolis: Fortress, 2003.

Lightfoot, J. B. *The Apostolic Fathers. Part I. S. Clement of Rome*. 2nd ed. Repr. Grand Rapids: Baker, 1981.

Martin, Dale B. *The Corinthian Body*. New Haven, CT: Yale University Press, 1995.

Meeks, Wayne A. *The First Urban Christians. The Social World of the Apostle Paul*. New Haven, CT: Yale University Press, 1983.

Murphy-O'Connor, Jerome. *St. Paul's Corinth. Texts and Archaeology*. Wilmington: Glazier; Collegeville, MN: Liturgical, 1983.

Papahatzis, Nicos. *Ancient Corinth. The Museums of Corinth, Isthmia and Sicyon*. Athens: Ekdotike Athenon S. A., 1981.

Robertson A. T., and A. Plummer, *A Critical and Exegetical Commentary on the First Epistle of St Paul to the Corinthians*. 2nd ed. Edinburgh: T. & T. Clark, 1914.

Sanders, Guy D. R., et al. *Ancient Corinth: A Guide to the Site and Museum*. 7th ed. Princeton, NJ: American School of Classical Studies at Athens, 2018.

Savage, Timothy B. *Power through Weakness: Paul's Understanding of the Christian Ministry in 2 Corinthians*. Cambridge: Cambridge University Press, 1996.

Theissen, Gerd. *The Social Setting of Pauline Christianity*. Philadelphia: Fortress, 1982.

Thiselton, Anthony C. *1 Corinthians. A Shorter Exegetical and Pastoral Commentary*. Grand Rapids: Eerdmans, 2006.

————. *The First Epistle to the Corinthians. A Commentary on the Greek Text*. Grand Rapids: Eerdmans/Carlisle: Paternoster, 2000.

Welborn, L. L. *Politics and Rhetoric in the Corinthian Epistles*. Macon, GA: Mercer University Press, 1977.

Winter, Bruce W. *Philo and Paul among the Sophists*. Cambridge: Cambridge University Press, 1997.

————. *After Paul Left Corinth: The Influence of Secular Ethics and Social Change*. Grand Rapids: Eerdmans, 2001.

Witherington, Ben, III. *Conflict and Community in Corinth*. Grand Rapids: Eerdmans, 1995.

———. *A Week in the Life of Corinth*. Downers Grove, IL: InterVarsity, 2012.

Part One:

Background

I. The City of Corinth

A. *History*

There are three important dates that form the background to Corinth in the first century AD. Each determined the cultural shape and distinctives of this city.

1. 146 BC: Destruction

Corinth's origin in the tenth century BC is shrouded in the mists of competing myths. But we know that in 243 BC it joined the Achaean League, a confederation of Greek city-states in the central and north-western parts of the Peloponnese. In 146 BC Corinth boldly rejected the third of three Roman embassies that aimed to end the ominous dispute between the League and Sparta, and then Corinth declared war on Sparta, Rome's ally. This prompted the Roman Republic under its general Lucius Mummius to lay siege to Corinth and finally destroy it. (This general was awarded the cognomen Achaicus to mark his final conquest and dissolution of the Achaean League). Corinth's male citizens were executed, women, children and freed slaves were all reduced to slavery, and the city's renowned wealth and treasures were plundered. Most if not all of the city's buildings were burned to the ground. As a result, for some one hundred years this celebrated icon of the Greek world lay in ruins, largely deserted except for an insignificant village.

2. 44 BC: Restoration

In the year 44 BC, now at the height of his power, Julius Caesar founded "the colony of Corinth in honor of the Julian dynasty" (*Colonia Laus Iulia Corinthiensis*) (see photo #1).

#1. The Temple of Octavia (=Temple E), the sister of the emperor Augustus, that was dedicated to the *gens Iulia,* the patrician family (including Julius Caesar) that founded Roman Corinth. Source credit: http://www. HolyLandPhotos.org.

As it happened, this founding occurred shortly before Caesar's assassination. Caesar's more practical motivation for this gesture of reconciliation towards Corinth was to provide an appropriate relocation for his veterans and for restless or ambitious freedmen and artisans in Rome, be they Roman, Greek, or Jewish. Plots of arable land in Corinth were made available for the new settlers. It has been estimated that by AD 50, some one hundred years later, the population of this cosmopolitan city had risen to some 50,000 people, largely due to its strategic geographical location (see Geography below) and the artistic energy of its city council that matched the generosity of its citizens who were vying for public recognition and honor. Corinth quickly became the proverbial "boom town" with hoardes of immigrants eager to capitalize on the manufacturing materials such as clay and bronze that were easily accessible locally and on the endless tourist traffic.

Evidence of the Romanization of Corinth may be found in several of the city's features.

- Most inscriptions were in Latin, not Greek
- The Roman theater in Corinth, rebuilt in the late first century BC, that later hosted gladiatorial shows (seating capacity about 14,000) (see photo #2)
- Several Corinthians or Corinthian inhabitants mentioned in the NT had Latin names (Titius Justus, Crispus, Fortunatus, Lucius, Gaius, Erastus, Quartus)
- Imperial cult activity (as in Temple E and the Julian Basilica)
- There was the minting of coins in Latin, although Greek influence continued with Aphrodite and Poseidon figuring prominently on the coins

#2. The semi-circular Corinthian theater.
After Paul's time it was used for wild beast and gladiatorial shows. Source credit: http://www.HolyLandPhotos.org.

3. 27 BC: Recognition

In this year the Emperor Augustus established Corinth as the capital of the Roman province of Achaia (= peninsular Greece). In spite of this imperial accolade, Corinth never eclipsed Athens as Greece's intellectual and educational center. If a Roman province was considered to be safe, it was under the control of the Senate as a senatorial colony; if it was likely to be the scene of political unrest or disturbance, it fell under the jurisdiction of the Emperor himself as an imperial colony with a permanent Roman garrison on site. Corinth began as a senatorial province, given the fact that many of its original inhabitants in 44 BC had served Rome under Julius Caesar or were loyal Roman citizens. But in AD 15 the Emperor Tiberius made Achaia an imperial province, while under Claudius it regained its senatorial status that it enjoyed during Paul's association with Corinth.

B. *Geography*

The site of ancient Corinth is about 3.5 miles southwest of modern (New) Corinth and about 50 miles west of Athens (see item #3).

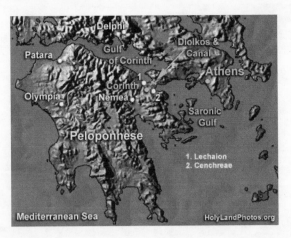

#3. Map of Southern Greece, showing the position of Corinth on the Isthmus and the two Corinthian ports of Lechaion (on the Gulf of Corinth) and Cenchreae (on the Saronic Gulf). Source credit: http://www.HolyLandPhotos.org.

One can scarcely overestimate the significance of the geographical location of ancient Corinth for its history and influence. It stood on a six-kilometer-wide elevated isthmus between northern Greece and the Peloponnese in the south, with two bustling ports—to the northwest there was Lechaion (Lechaeum) on the inland Gulf of Corinth that served trade routes from Italy and Sicily, while to the east was Cenchreae on the Saronic Gulf that led to Asia. Strabo spoke of Corinth as "master of two harbors" (*Geography* 8.6.20). Situated, then, at the strategic intersection between north and south and between east and west, the city naturally became a center for unparalleled commercial prosperity and ascendancy as well as for tourism. Merchant ships traveling from west to east preferred to use the convenience of the *diolkos* across the isthmus (see Archaeology below) in spite of the toll fees and taxes on goods in transit rather than risk the treacherous 200-mile/six-day journey around Cape Malea at the southern tip of the Peloponnese, the scene of Beaufort Force 6 gales and many shipwrecks. Clear evidence of the strategic importance of this east-west passage are the repeated plans or attempts from the earliest times to create a canal (of 3.9 miles) across the isthmus—a goal not finally achieved until 1881–1893 (see photo #4).

#4. The modern Corinth Canal, constructed by a French engineering company during 1881–1893. Source credit: http://www.HolyLandPhotos.org.

Towering behind the city at 574 meters was the steep, majestic Acrocorinth (see photo #5).

#5. The seven monolithic Doric columns of the Temple of Apollo, dating from the decade after 550 BC, with the Acrocorinth in the background. Source credit: http://www.HolyLandPhotos.org.

In times of conflict this mountain was a virtually impregnable fortress, with its three massive man-made walls and gates on the accessible west side, its almost inexhaustible water supply from the Peirene Fountains, and its commanding view of the entrance to the Peloponnese. In pre-destruction Corinth the temple of Aphrodite, the goddess of love, stood at the top of the Acrocorinth, and it "owned" multitudes of temple-slave prostitutes (who presumably operated mainly in the city), according to Strabo (*Geography* 8.6.20).

C. *Archaeology*

There are at least six archaeological finds at Corinth that shed light on the city in the first century AD and Paul's Corinthian letters.

1. *The Gallio Inscription (see photo #6)*

#6. The Gallio Inscription (in Greek) from Delphi, with Gallio's name (ΓΑΛΛΙΩΝ) visible on the fourth line from the top. Source credit: http://www.HolyLandPhotos.org.

In Acts 18:1–17 Luke recounts an incident "while Gallio was proconsul of Achaia" in which local Jews brought Paul before the proconsul's "judgment seat" or "tribunal" (*bema*) and charged him with "persuading the people to worship God in ways contrary to the law" (= Roman law) (Acts 18:12–13). Without even giving Paul an opportunity to respond to this charge, Gallio refused to adjudicate the case since it involved merely questions about words and names and interpretations of Jewish law, and then he paid no attention to a display of anti-Semitism when the crowd beat Sosthenes, the leader of the synagogue, in front of the *bema* (see below).

Lucius Junius Gallio served as Roman proconsul at Corinth, then a senatorial province, probably from July AD 51 to July AD 52. We can be confident about these dates because of a Latin inscription that may be dated in the first months of AD 52:

"Tiberius Claudius Caesar Augustus Germanicus, Pontifex Maximus, in the 12th year of his tribunate, acclaimed emperor for the 26th time, father of his country, consul for the fifth time, censor, greets the city of Delphi. I have already for a long time felt affection for the city of Delphi, being kindly disposed towards it from the beginning and I have always observed the cult of the Pythian Apollo, but concerning the present tidings and the quarrels of citizens about which Lucius Junius Gallio, my friend and proconsul of Achaia [= Greece], informs me . . . will still maintain the boundaries as formerly marked out."

We may date this rescript of Claudius as falling between January 25, AD 51 (= the beginning of Claudius's eleventh year, when the twenty-second and twenty-fourth "acclamations" were held) and August 1, AD 52 (before which the twenty-seventh "acclamation" had been held). Accordingly, the twenty-sixth "acclamation" occurred probably in the first seven months of AD 52, so that this inscription belongs to early AD 52. Since the boundary dispute alluded to would have taken time to be investigated and reported to Claudius in Rome for a verdict, the imperial rescript was probably received during the second half of Gallio's term of office which ran from July to July. His proconsulship may therefore be dated, with high probability, as occurring from July AD 51 to July AD 52.

This inscription is also helpful in dating Paul's initial residence in Corinth. Working from Luke's sequence of events in Acts 18—viz. 18 months (v. 11), Gallio episode (vv. 12–17), "many days/ some time" (v. 18)—we may tentatively date Paul's first sojourn in Corinth as Fall 50–Spring 52.

In its significance for the Christian mission at Corinth and elsewhere in the Roman empire, this Gallio episode was profoundly important.

It meant that Paul could not be accused of infringing any Roman law by his aggressive ministry. On the contrary, the freedom enjoyed by Jews under Roman law as participants in a "legal religion" (*religio licita*) had now been implicitly granted to Christians who were viewed by the Romans as being a Jewish sect. Paul could continue his Corinthian ministry unopposed by Roman authority and his previous eighteen months of ministry were legally validated. What is more, after Paul's departure, the Corinthian church could assume Roman protection from Jewish interference. And even after Gallio's departure from office, Christians elsewhere could appeal to the Corinthian precedent for protection; after all, the emperor was a "friend" of Gallio!

2. The Erastus Inscription (see photo #7)

#7. The Erastus inscription (in Latin) still visible on the site of Ancient Corinth. Source credit: http://www.HolyLandPhotos.org.

On a large square pavement (laid about AD 50) adjacent to the entrance to the Roman amphitheatre, archaeologists discovered in 1929 a brief inscription engraved on a slab of Acrocorinthian limestone. It reads "ERASTUS PRO AED[ILITATE] S[UA] P[ECUNIA] STRAVIT," "Erastus laid (this pavement) at his own expense, in return for (his appointment to) the aedileship."

This Erastus may confidently be identified with the man mentioned in Rom 16:13 (written from Corinth early in AD 57): "Erastus, the city's director of public works, and our brother Quartus send you their greetings." Whether we translate the (Greek) phrase *ho oikonomos tēs poleōs* as "the city's director of public works" (NIV) or "the city's treasurer" (NRSV), Erastus held high public office as the *aedile*, who was a regularly elected business manager (and judge) for the city council, responsible for the main-tenance of public places and buildings. To hold this position was a remarkable achievement for a Christian in a cosmopolitan city such as Roman Corinth. Erastus himself would have been wealthy (note "at his own expense"). A person of comparable high status was Phoebe at the nearby church of Cenchreae, whom Paul calls a "patroness" (*prostatis*, Rom 16:1–2).

Although important public officials were required to pledge their loyalty to Jupiter and the divine emperor, when Gallio's ver-dict effectively made Christianity a "legal religion" (see the Gallio inscription above), Christians involved in civic affairs may have become exempt from making this pledge.

3. *The Synagogue Inscription (see photo #8)*

#8. The partially preserved Synagogue Inscription (in Greek), indirect evidence of the presence of Jews in Corinth during Paul's time. Source credit: http://www.HolyLandPhotos.org.

The size of the Jewish population in Corinth in Paul's time is unknown. There is no direct archaeological evidence for a synagogue such as is mentioned in Acts 18:4 but dating from a later time (fourth century AD) is a partially preserved (Greek) inscription found on the Lechaion Road by the steps leading into the agora. It reads: [ΣΥΝ]ΑΓωΓΗΕΒΡ[ΑΙωΝ], "Synagogue of the Hebrews" (= Jews), and probably was built over the synagogue of Paul's time, as was the Jewish custom.

4. The Bema (see photo #9)

#9. The elevated Bema ("judicial bench") in the Forum, with the Acrocorinth in the background. Source credit: http://www.HolyLandPhotos.org.

In the discussion of the Gallio inscription above, we sketched Luke's account of Paul's arraignment before the proconsul. There Luke refers three times to the *bema* (Acts 18:12, 16–17), variously translated as "judgment seat" (KJV, NASB), "judicial bench" (Cassirer), "judge's bench" (HCSB), "tribunal" (NAB, NRSV, ESV), or, in an effort to give a modern equivalent, "court" (NIV) or "courtroom" (NLT). It was the elevated speaker's platform in front of the proconsul's residence where he heard legal cases and delivered his verdicts. It was also the venue for public ceremonies.

In 1935 archaeologists discovered this elevated *bema* on the south side of the *agora*, the city's "market place" that was about

200 meters long and 100 meters wide. This *agora* was surrounded by rows of shops, temples and offices and it formed the commercial and administrative nerve center of the city. Appropriately, the Greek text of Acts 18:12–17 is displayed at the site of the *bema*.

5. *The Diolkos (see photo #10)*

#10. A section of the Diolkos, showing the tracks for the wheeled vessels used to haul small ships across the Isthmus. Source credit: http://www. HolyLandPhotos.org.

Dating from the sixth century BC, and partly parallel to the modern Corinthian canal that stretches between the two harbors, was the *diolkos*. This was a stone track or paved roadway 3 to 5.5 meters wide that was perhaps first used for military purposes but then was used to transport goods or drag small vessels across the isthmus. The technical term derives from the basic verb *helkō* ("drag") and the preposition *dia* (here "across") and from the compound form *dielkō* ("pull through," "haul across"). Ships first unloaded their cargo that would be transported overland by oxen to the opposite port. Then the ships themselves were strapped to wheeled vehicles called "haulers of ships" (*holkoi neōn*) for the passage across the *diolkos*.

This *diolkos* is clear testimony to the vibrancy of east-west trade from Italy to Asia through Corinth and the city's consequent opulence.

6. The Isthmian Games

The Isthmian Games were held in honor of Poseidon, the god of the sea, every two years in the spring at Isthmia which is about ten miles east of ancient Corinth. These Games were second in importance only to the Olympic Games that were held every four years. Participants and spectators from across the Roman Empire flooded into Corinth for a wide range of competitive events—not only chariot races and a wide range of athletic events, but also musical competitions in trumpet, flute and lyre, poetry reading, and even contests for women. This sudden influx of people who needed rooms to rent, food to eat, and exotic mementos to buy, presented endless opportunities for commercial entrepreneurs who provided porters, guides, entertainers, accountants, cooks, craftsmen and tentmakers along with a myriad of other services.

There can be little doubt that Paul timed his sojourn in Corinth to coincide neatly with these biennial pan-Hellenic games that would provide a wide audience for his preaching. If Paul's arrival in Corinth may be dated in the Fall of AD 50 (see above under the Gallio inscription), he would have been busy along with Aquila and Priscilla (Acts 18:2–3) for several months plying their trade of making and repairing canvas and leather tents and awnings, probably on the Lechaion Road (see photo #11), for the swarm of visitors coming in the Spring of AD 51 when the Games were held.

#11. The paved Lechaion Road, with its paved footpaths edged with gutters that collected the rainwater, led north from the Forum to the port of Lechaion. The Acrocorinth is in the background. Source credit: http://www.HolyLandPhotos.org.

D. *Corinthian Society and the Infant Corinthian church*

An accurate picture of the principal characteristics of the inhabitants of the city of Corinth in the first century AD may be drawn up on the basis of archaeological finds including contemporary inscriptions, and especially the observations of first and second century AD writers, such as the Greek authors Strabo, Dio Chrysostom, Aristides, and Epictetus, and Roman writers such as Livy, Pliny the Younger, Suetonius, Seneca, Apuleius, Tacitus, and Petronius.

We may summarize those characteristics as follows.

1. Tolerance of plurality, probably a corollary of the cosmopolitan nature of the city. Most Corinthians adopted a "live and let live" attitude toward their fellow citizens: everyone was entitled to their distinctive worldview and lifestyle choices, whatever their status in life and whatever gods they worshiped (there were more than thirty cults and more than twelve temples or shrines in Corinth at this time).

For Paul and his fellow Christians, simply living in Corinth demanded a certain degree of tolerance, since interacting with residents on a daily basis was inevitable. But alongside this necessary tolerance was an intolerance of the omnipresent licentiousness, such as the sexual advances of homosexuals or prostitutes. "Shun sexual immorality" (1 Cor 6:18). In 1 Cor 5:9–10 Paul refers to an earlier letter (see III. A. below) in which he implored his fellow believers "not to associate with sexually immoral people—not at all meaning the people of this world who are immoral, or the greedy and swindlers, or idolaters, since you would then need to leave this world." In a nutshell, they were to be in but not of the world; there was both the inevitable compatibility and a rigorous exclusivity. Moreover, all Corinthian believers, whatever their nationality ("Jews or Gentiles") or social status ("slave or free") were one in Christ (1 Cor 12:13) and could be addressed corporately as *adelphoi*, "brothers and sisters" (twenty times in 1 Cor and three times in 2 Cor) and as *agapētoi*, "dear friends" (twice in 1 Cor and twice in 2 Cor).

These dual themes—inevitable involvement and yet necessary difference—are not explicitly evident in 1 Clement but are certainly implied in the review of the Corinthians' outlook, behavior and reputation found in the first two chapters. And in this letter, too, the recipients are regularly addressed corporately as *adelphoi* (fourteen times) and *agapētoi* (seventeen times).

2. *Patent inequality*, in spite of a general upward mobility among the inhabitants. A chasm naturally developed between the relatively few wealthy aristocrats, perhaps 5 percent of the population, and the more numerous menial slaves who struggled to survive. Between these two extremes were a middle class of diligent citizens who longed and worked for higher social status. The infant church in Corinth, representing a cross-section of society, reflected these same tensions. "When you were called, not many of you were wise by human standards; not many held positions of influence; not many were of noble birth" (1 Cor 1:26). Slaves were present in the Corinthian church (1 Cor 7:21–22), as were at least two heads of households that would have included slaves—Stephanas (1 Cor

1:16) and Crispus (Acts 18:8), not to mention Erastus, the wealthy and high-ranking city official (see C. 2 above).

This inequality may have been illustrated by the circumstances of the *agape*-meal and the Lord's Supper at Corinth (1 Cor 11:17–22) that did "more harm than good" (1 Cor 11:17b). If Roman banquet customs were followed at these meetings, the more well-to-do believers may have reclined on couches in the *triclinium* (dining room) of the house and enjoyed superior food and drink, while the more menial members were gathered far less comfortably in the *atrium* (hallway) with inferior provisions or even the leftovers. Such a situation would account for the details of the apostle's indictment in 1 Cor 11:21–22: "When you are eating, some of you go ahead with your own private suppers. As a result, one person goes hungry and another gets drunk. What! Don't you have homes to eat and drink in? Or do you show contempt for the church of God by humiliating those who have nothing?"

Paul himself was the opposite of the social climber. He refused monetary support from those to whom he was currently ministering, thus rejecting the patronage scheme by which money was transferred to those lower on the social scale in return for recognition. He may have been regarded as "weak" (cf. 1 Cor 4:9–13; 2 Cor 6:10b; 10:1, 10; 11:27) or socially inferior as a tradesperson working and living along the Lechaion Road with Aquila and Priscilla (Acts 18:2–3).

Explicit reference to the societal extremes of freemen and slaves are lacking in 1 Clement, where the contrast is between the young who initiated the revolt and the "elders" or "bishops" who were deposed (3:3; 44:4). These elders had gained a reputation for exercising their gifts "blamelessly and in holiness" (44:4) "for a long time" (44:3). This being so, it is fair to assume that they were drawn from the more prominent strata of society, probably being heads of households that would have included slaves. Yet all members of the church were encouraged to recognize their equality as "the members of Christ and . . . members of one another" (46:7) and as corporately forming "the flock of Christ" (44:3; 54:2) and a "brotherhood" (2:4; 47:5; 48:1) that was given to hospitality (1:2; 11:1; 12:1, 3).

3. *Craze for adulation*, prompted by an urge to excel. Winners at the Isthmian Games were treated as permanent heroes and they revelled in their universal acclaim. After all, they were "first of those in the inhabited world." Victory was publicized in inscriptions, especially if superiority was maintained: "Isthmia twice . . . Olympia three times." If a person excelled over their rivals, whether in running, banking, acting, business or rhetoric, they became famous. Adulation could also be attained by an impressive personal appearance and by outstanding rhetorical skills.

The city's most well-known benefactor was Gnaeus Babbius Philinus, probably a liberated slave of Greek descent originally from Rome. He was immortalized by the impressive Babbius Monument, with its eight Corinthian columns in a circle, that stood in the agora. It was erected, his inscription (see photo #12) tells us, "at his own expense, and he approved it in his official capacity as *duovir*," one of two chief magistrates.

#12. The Babbius Inscription (in Latin), a testimony to one of Corinth's most distinguished citizens and benefactors. Source credit: http://www. HolyLandPhotos.org.

Against this background of vigorous competitiveness and boasting about personal achievements, Paul encouraged the Corinthians to follow his own example (1 Cor 4:16) of humble, sacrificial service for others (1 Cor 4:11–13; 2 Cor 6:4–6; 11:23–27). "Love does not brag, is not full of its own importance" (1 Cor 13:4). When Paul himself was forced to indulge in some "foolish boasting" to match his opponents' boasting (2 Cor 11:16–18), he did so with great reluctance (2 Cor 11:21b; 12:11) and chose to boast about whatever displayed his weakness (2 Cor 11:30; 12:9–10).

There is a recurrent call in 1 Clement for humility (e.g., 16:2, 17; 21:8; 30:2–3, 8; 52:4; 59:3). This implies a rejection of the pursuit of recognition and status: "Christ belongs to those who are humble, not to those who exalt themselves over his flock" (16:1).

4. *Pursuit of wealth* that was readily available to those committed to personal enterprise and hard work. Commercial entrepreneurs would have been fully aware of the ideal circumstances for financial returns afforded by the flourishing city:

- A sizeable population of about 50,000, swollen by a regular influx of sailors, and by those attending the Isthmian Games every second year;

- Corinth was a renowned center for religious pilgrimage and tourism;

- There were plentiful natural resources, including many freshwater springs (see photo #13), for industry such as pottery and ceramics;

- Skilled slave labor was always available for maintenance of roads and buildings, and specialized tasks such as building and repairing ships; a businessman who owned a fleet of merchant ships would quickly become a millionaire;

- Predictable income came from transit fees for transporting goods and ships across the Isthmus.

#13. Behind the six arches of this Lower Peirene Fountain were four reservoirs forming the city's main water supply. Source credit: http://www. HolyLandPhotos.org.

As Paul encouraged generous Corinthian contributions to his aid for the poor in Jerusalem, he directed them to "store up some money in proportion to how you are prospering" (1 Cor 16:2) and spoke of their "plenty" at the present time and of his goal of equality of supply of the necessities of life (2 Cor 8:13–14).

1 Clement has a single admonition on this matter. "The Holy Spirit says: 'Let the wise man not boast about his wisdom, nor the strong man about his strength, nor the rich about his wealth; but let the person who boasts, boast in the Lord'" (13.1; alluding to Jer 9:23–24; cf. 1 Cor 1:31; 2 Cor 10:17).

5. *Preoccupation with personal physical pleasure,* whether this be brought about by feasting (witness the abundance of taverns and the frequency of banquets in temples) or by sexual adventure, all at the expense of intellectual pursuits. The reestablishment of Corinth in 44 BC simply confirmed the reputation of pre-146 BC Corinth for licentiousness (see the reference to Strabo's claim mentioned at B. above). So entrenched was this reputation that it was reflected

in two coinages in the Greek language: the verb *corinthiazesthai*
("to corinthianize") was polite Greek for "practice immorality" or
"lead a dissolute life," while *corinthia korē* ("Corinthian girl") was
a euphemism for a prostitute.

In 1978 one of my students gave me a record of a 1976 guided
tour in the Archaeological Museum of Corinth. In a narrow room
adjacent to the Hall of Asclepieion, not normally accessible to visitors, were grotesque sculptures evidencing the ravaging effects of
venereal diseases on all parts of the human body.

Little wonder, then, that Paul addressed the issue of incest
in 1 Cor 5:1–13 and sexual immorality in 1 Cor 6:12–20 after
saying "Neither the sexually immoral nor idolaters nor adulter-
ers nor those involved in pederasty or sodomy . . . will inherit the
kingdom of God. And that is what some of you used to be" (1 Cor
6:9–11). Paul called for a ruthless stop to the dissolute Corinthian
lifestyle: "Expel the wicked man from your community" (1 Cor
5:13). "Keep well clear of sexual immorality" (1 Cor 6:18). Also
significant is the fact that Paul wrote the book of Romans with its
indictment of sexual depravity (Rom 1:18–27) while he was living
in Corinth.

So far from being preoccupied with personal satisfaction
of every type, a person "ought to seek the common advantage of
all, and not his own" (1 Clem 48:6) and "be zealous to do good"
(34:2; cf. 8:4; 33:1). In particular, believers should "do all the things
that promote holiness, forsaking slander, abominable and impure
embraces, drunkenness and rioting and detestable desires, foul
adultery, and detestable pride" (30:1; cf. 21:7; 28:1; 29:1).

Part Two:

The Apostle Paul and Corinth

I. Paul's Three Visits to Corinth

A. *The Founding Visit* (Acts 18:1–18)

Paul describes his personal circumstances at the time of this visit in 1 Cor 2:1–5. Arriving from Athens (v. 1), he came "in weakness, with timidity and great trembling" (v. 3). He chose to avoid manipulative rhetoric (vv. 1, 4) lest the Corinthians' faith should rest on human cleverness (v. 5), preferring to focus on a cross-centered presentation of the gospel (v. 2).

Luke's account of Paul's founding of the church at Corinth is found in Acts 18:1–18. What can we deduce from that account about the characteristics of that church?

1. Two of its founding members were hospitable local tradespeople—*Aquila and Priscilla.*

This couple had recently arrived from Italy because of the Emperor Claudius's edict of AD 49 that all Jews must leave Rome (Acts 18:2). Although the Roman biographer Suetonius refers to this edict (*Claudius* 25), only the fifth-century historian Orosius (*History* 7.6.15–16) dates it—in the ninth year of Claudius's reign, viz. January 25, AD 49 to January 24, AD 50.[1]

---

1. See further, Murray J. Harris, *Three Crucial Questions About Jesus*

In several regards Aquila and Priscilla were an exemplary couple to whom Paul could appeal as a model for their fellow believers in Corinth to follow.

(i) *In all probability they formed a mixed marriage, Jew and Gentile.* Verse 2 indicates that Aquila (Latin for "eagle") was a Jew and a native of Pontus, a Roman province situated on the southern side of the Black Sea. It is unlikely he had been a slave in Pontus, for the inscriptional evidence indicates that "Aquila" was not ordinarily a slave name. Perhaps this refugee Jewish tentmaker had become a Christian in Pontus as the result of the testimony of Jewish pilgrims from Pontus who had been in Jerusalem at Pentecost (Acts 2:9).

Luke prefers the name Priscilla (Acts 18:2, 18, 26), a conversational form of Prisca which is Paul's preference (Rom 16:3; 1 Cor 16:19; 2 Tim 4:19). It is improbable that Priscilla was a Jewess, for Luke simply adds the unqualified "with his wife Priscilla" (Acts 18:2). Given her formal name, Prisca (not usually a slave name), Priscilla may well have been related in some way to the renowned Roman family, the *gens Prisca.*

(ii) *They were devoted to one another in Christian marriage.* If Prisca was a freeborn Roman, she was under no obligation to leave Rome because of the emperor's edict, but she did so with her Jewish husband. Moreover, she followed her husband's craft; the plurals "them" and "they" in Acts 18:2 and 3 refer to both Aquila and Priscilla. This illustrates their compatibility and co-operation. Also, Aquila was apparently not offended by Priscilla's greater visibility and probably greater giftedness that are shown by the fact that, exceptionally (given first-century practice), she is mentioned before Aquila in four of the six references to the joint pair (Acts 18:18, 26; Rom 16:3; 2 Tim 4:19).

(iii) *They were given to hospitality.* Paul not only worked along-side Priscilla and Aquila in their leather-working business,

(Eugene, OR: Wipf & Stock, 2008) 21–24.

but also "lived with" or "lodged" ("abode," KJV) with them (Acts 18:3). From 1 Cor 16:19 (written from Ephesus) we know that one of the Ephesian household churches met in their house and Paul singles out Aquila and Priscilla among "all the brothers and sisters" in Ephesus (1 Cor 16:20) as giving greetings to the Corinthians (1 Cor 16:19), probably because he was "staying as a guest" with them (as some Western textual witnesses add) and because they were well loved by their friends in Corinth. Also here at Ephesus they wisely took Apollos aside to their home and "explained to him the way of God more adequately" (Acts 18:26). At Rome also these tentmakers made their home a "tent of meeting" for the Lord's people. "Give my greetings also to the church that meets at their house" (Rom 16:5). It may have been this couple who wrote the letter from Ephesus to the Corinthian believers that encouraged them to give Apollos a warm welcome when he arrived (Acts 18:27).

(iv) *They were willing to risk their lives for the sake of the gospel.* In Rom 16:3–16 Prisca and Aquila head the list of twenty-six named fellow believers in Rome whom Paul greets. Of this couple he says, they "once risked their necks for me" (Rom 16:4). While the expression refers literally to the exposing of the neck to the executioner's sword, here it is a metaphor for complete exposure to mortal danger. When this occurred we do not know. It may have been when Paul's life was in danger at Corinth (cf. Acts 18:6, 10, 12) or when he faced man-shaped beasts in Ephesus (1 Cor 15:32; cf. Acts 20:19) or during the Demetrius riot at Ephesus (Acts 19:23–41).

2. Central to the infant church's creed at Corinth must have been belief in the messiahship of Jesus of Nazareth. At the outset of his ministry there Paul argued in the synagogue every Sabbath and tried to convince Jews and Greeks (Acts 18:4). After the arrival of Silas and Timothy from Macedonia, Paul "began to give himself exclusively to preaching, testifying to the Jews that *Jesus*

is the Messiah" (Acts 18:5). But because of Jewish opposition and slander he turned his evangelistic focus to the Gentiles, meeting in the house of Titius Justus adjacent to the synagogue (Acts 18:6–7).

In the early church two affirmations about Jesus were foundational for its basis of faith: "Jesus is the Messiah" (Acts 18:5) and "Jesus is Lord" (1 Cor 12:3). Clearly the former affirmation was at the heart of Paul's apologetic in the synagogue at Corinth, as it had been at Thessalonica (Acts 17:3). It was established by Paul through reasoning "from the Scriptures" (Acts 17:2), that is, by apologetic appeal to Scriptural prophecy, by showing that Jesus of Nazareth fulfilled the biblical predictions about God's promised Messiah. This practice of proving from the Scriptures that "Jesus is the Messiah" was continued at Corinth by Apollos who "powerfully refuted his Jewish opponents in public debate" (Acts 18:28).

The other affirmation, "Jesus is Lord," would have been justified by appeal to the evidence for Jesus's resurrection from the dead to the place of highest honor in the universe as God's plenipotentiary (cf. Acts 17:3, 31).

3. *Jewish opposition to Paul at Corinth seems to have progressed in two stages.* At first, the opposition was *verbal,* with most of the Jews rejecting his message of the messiahship of Jesus and abusing him, probably as an apostate Jew (Acts 18:5b–6a). In response Paul "shook out his clothes," a symbolic act (cf. Acts 13:51) that exempted him from responsibility for their response, and he declared that his principal evangelistic focus (cf. Acts 18:19) from now on would be among the Gentiles (Acts 18:6). Accordingly, he left the synagogue and thereafter the house of Titius Justus, a "God-fearing" Gentile, apparently became the first house church in Corinth for believers such as Crispus and his whole household (Acts 18:7–8).

In its second stage, the opposition was *physical.* Acting in a united front ("with a single impulse"), the Jews laid hands on Paul and forcibly brought him into the marketplace where the Roman tribunal (the *bēma*) was situated (Acts 18:12). The previous assurance of the Lord Jesus in a vision was simply that no physical *harm* would come to him in Corinth, not that all opposition would cease (Acts 18:9–10). On the nature and significance of this Gallio episode (Acts 18:12–17), see above C. 1.

B. *The "Painful (or Intermediate) Visit"*

1. *Its Historicity*

In 2 Cor 12:14 and 13:1–2 Paul refers to two prior visits he had made to Corinth, and he indicates in 2 Cor 2:1 and 12:21 that one of these two earlier visits proved to be painful. We cannot imagine that he would ever have summarized his successful founding visit recorded in Acts 18:1–17 as being "painful" (*en lypē*, 2:1), although he faced vigorous opposition at that time (Acts 18:6, 9–10, 12).

2. *Its Time*

Since 1 Corinthians presupposes only one previous visit, the founding visit (1 Cor 2:1–5; 3:1–3, 6, 10; 11:2, 23) although a second visit is announced (1 Cor 4:18–19, 21; 11:34; 16:2–3, 5–7), the "painful" visit mentioned in 2 Corinthians may be assumed to have occurred between the writing on these two letters; hence its other name, "the intermediate visit." It seems highly unlikely that Paul would have revived painful memories in 2 Corinthians after ignoring or forgetting them in 1 Corinthians.

3. *Its Occasion, Purpose, and Outcome*

For reasons that remain unclear, the situation in the church at Corinth deteriorated after 1 Corinthians was received there. There may have been tension about the implementing of the apostle's directive about ejecting the incestuous man from the congregation (1 Cor 5:2, 5, 13), with a group of ultra-loyal Paulinists (see 1 Cor

1:12; 2 Cor 2:6–7) advocating one course of action, and an influ-ential anti-Pauline clique of intruders from Palestine, the "false apostles" (2 Cor 11:13–15), espousing a different approach.

On receiving adverse news about the situation, perhaps from Timothy, Paul apparently hurried to Corinth to reinforce his ad-monitions in 1 Corinthians and prevent any further undermining of his authority. He seems to have rebuked those guilty of immo-rality ("those who sinned earlier," 2 Cor 12:21; 13:2) but stopped short of exercising summary discipline, choosing rather to give a warning: "I already gave you a warning when I was present on my second visit. I now repeat it while absent: 'On my return I will not spare (you)'" (2 Cor 13:2). Also, he says that God humiliated him on this second visit ("again" [*palin*] belongs with "humiliate" in 2 Cor 12:21), perhaps because the Corinthians' failed to side with him decisively against the false apostles.

At some point after this brief, painful visit, Paul or possibly his representative was insulted by some nameless individual at Corinth in an open act of defiance by which all the Corinthians were to some extent pained—if not at the actual time, at least later on (2 Cor 2:5–11). As a result Paul sent Titus to Corinth after con-siderable persuasion (2 Cor 7:14) as his personal envoy to deliver the "severe letter" (on which see III. C. below).[2]

C. *The Final Visit* (Acts 20:2–3)

Paul's promised third visit to Corinth, mentioned six times at the end of 2 Corinthians (12:14, 20–21; 13:1–2, 10), took place after he had traveled through Macedonia, "giving many encouraging mes-sages to the people" there (Acts 20:1–2). He spent three months in Greece (= primarily Corinth) (Acts 20:3a), the winter of AD 56–57. If the overarching purpose of 2 Corinthians was to pave the way for a trouble-free and mutually advantageous visit (see 2 Cor 12:14–15, 19; 13:9–10), this seemed to have been achieved, in

---

2. For a detailed defense of these views about the "painful visit," see Murray J. Harris, *The Second Epistle to the Corinthians: A Commentary on the Greek Text* (Grand Rapids: Eerdmans/Milton Keynes: Paternoster, 2005), 54–59.

spite of and perhaps because of his dire warnings (2 Cor 12:20–21; 13:2–4). There are three reasons for assuming this positive outcome.

(i) Toward the end of this three-month sojourn in Corinth, Paul wrote or completed his letter to the Roman church (early AD 57). In Romans Paul expresses some apprehension about the future (Rom 15:30–31) but none about the present, and he would hardly be contemplating fulfilling his long-standing desire to visit Rome (Rom 1:10–11, 13, 15; 15:22–24, 28–29, 32) and undertaking pioneer evangelism in the west (Rom 15:20–21, 23–24, 28) if the congregation in the city from which he was writing was still harboring his opponents who espoused a false gospel and were exploiting the Corinthians (2 Cor 11:4, 20).

(ii) Paul would hardly have said that Achaia (= Corinth) was "pleased" to make a contribution to his collection for the poor in Jerusalem (Rom 15:26–27) unless the Corinthians were in harmony with the promoter of the collection.

(iii) The very preservation of 2 Corinthians as an apostolic letter is evidence that Paul's contest with his adversaries turned out successfully.

II. Paul's Four Letters to Corinth

A. The "Previous Letter" (1 Cor 5:9–10)

In the course of dealing with the case of incest within the church
(1 Cor 5:1–13), Paul reminds the Corinthians "I wrote to you in
the letter not to associate indiscriminately with sexually immoral
people" (1 Cor 5:9). Apparently some had taken that to mean that
all association with unbelievers should be avoided. Paul now corrects this misunderstanding by saying, "—not of course meaning
total dissociation from the immoral people of this world, or the
greedy or swindlers or idolaters, for in that case you would have
to withdraw totally from the world" (1 Cor 5:10). He is calling for
discrimination in social relations so as to maintain the purity of
the church fellowship.

In the phrase "in the letter" (*en tē epistolē*) the Greek article
denotes possession, so the meaning is "(I wrote to you) in *my* letter," not "In the present letter (that I am writing to you)." This earlier document, no longer extant, is regularly called "the previous
letter." What prompted Paul to write the letter, and who delivered
it, is unknown. Since it preceded 1 Corinthians that was written
from Ephesus (1 Cor 16:9), it probably originated from that city.
Certainly it was written after Acts 18:18 but before Acts 20:2–3.

B. *1 Corinthians* (see VI below)

C. *The "Severe Letter"* (2 Cor 2:3–4)

"The letter I wrote you arose from intense affliction and anguish
of heart and amid many tears, not to cause you pain but to let you
know how deeply I love you" (2 Cor 2:4). This is Paul's description
of what has come to be known as the "severe letter," the "letter of
tears," or the "sorrowful/painful letter."

Some unknown time after Paul's "painful visit" (see II. B.
above) and return to Ephesus, news reached him that he or possibly his representative had been seriously and publicly defamed or

attacked in the Corinthian church. This unexpected development, along with memories of the earlier unpleasant visit, caused him tearful anguish (2 Cor 2:4) and led to his writing of a stern letter that was delivered by his envoy, Titus. We can establish its purpose and effect from Titus's report to Paul (2 Cor 7:6–16).

1. *Its Purpose*

The overall aim of the letter was to arouse the church to discipline "the one who committed the offence" (2 Cor 7:12; cf. 2:6) and thus, incidentally, vindicate "the injured party" (7:12; = Paul himself). The apostle mentions other purposes: (1) to avoid another "painful visit" (2 Cor 1:23–2:4); (2) to show his deep affection for the Corinthians (2 Cor 2:4); (3) to test the Corinthians' obedience to his authority (2 Cor 2:9); (4) to make clear to them in the sight of God their actual devotion to him (2 Cor 7:12)—with the benefit of hindsight Paul states this as his main purpose.

2. *Its Effect*

(i) On the Corinthians

According to Titus (2 Cor 7:6–16) the Corinthians as a whole felt deep sorrow, concern and alarm over their behavior during the "painful visit." They wanted to assure Paul in person of their change of attitude; they were now indignant about the offender's action and were eager to punish him, as shown by the penalty they had inflicted on him (2 Cor 2:6).

(ii) On Paul

Paul's initial reaction on hearing Titus's report was to feel regret that he had caused his converts pain by his letter, but on reflection his viewpoint had changed and he now felt no regret because the unavoidable pain had proved remedial. God had been at work—their pain had providentially produced their repentance and necessary action, so that now they were innocent in the whole matter.

3. *Its Identification*

Scholars who believe that 2 Corinthians combines originally separate letters sometimes identify 2 Cor 10–13 as the main part of the "severe letter." More common, however, is the proposal that this letter is actually 1 Corinthians, so that "the wrongdoer" (2 Cor 7:12) is the incestuous man (1 Cor 5:1) and "the injured party" (2 Cor 7:12) is this man's father.

For several reasons this popular identification is highly improbable. (1) 1 Corinthians does not deal primarily with the wrongdoer and the need for his punishment, as 2 Cor 2:6, 9 seems to demand. (2) Would Paul personally offer to forgive a man guilty of incest (2 Cor 2:10)? (3) Would not even the Corinthians have been scandalized by one of their church members living with his stepmother while his father was still alive? (4) 2 Cor 1:23; 2:1, 3 indicates that this "severe letter" was written in place of another painful visit, which is hardly true of 1 Corinthians (see, e.g., 1 Cor 4:18–19; 11:34; 16:2–3, 5–7).

These two unlikely identifications lead us to conclude that this letter, like the "previous letter," in no longer extant. Its non-preservation is hardly surprising since the letter would have been intensely personal, quite brief, and addressed to a specific unedifying situation.

D. *2 Corinthians* (see VII below)

III. Chart Showing the Relationship
of the Visits and the Letters

Visits	Letters
1. *Founding visit* of 18+ months (Fall 50—Spring AD 52), from Athens (Acts 18:1–18a)	
	1. *"Previous Letter"* (1 Cor 5:9–11) probably sent from Ephesus; not extant; bearer and date unknown
	2. *1 Corinthians* sent from Ephesus (1 Cor 16:8–9) in Spring AD 55 (1 Cor 5:7–8; 16:8); probably delivered by the three-man deputation from Corinth (1 Cor 16:12, 17)
2. Short *"painful visit,"* from and returning to Ephesus, in Summer or Fall AD 55 (2 Cor 2:1; 12:14, 21; 13:1–2)	
	3. *"Severe Letter"* (2 Cor 2:3–4, 9; 7:8, 12) sent from Ephesus in Spring AD 56; not extant; delivered by Titus (2 Cor 2:12–13; 7:5–16)
	4. *2 Corinthians* sent from Macedonia (2 Cor 7:5; 8:1–5; 9:1–4) in Fall AD 56; delivered by Titus and his two colleagues (2 Cor 8:17–18, 22)

3. *Final visit, of three months*
   (Winter AD 56–57), from
   Macedonia (Acts 20:1–3),
   during which time Paul wrote
   his letter to the Romans (Rom
   16:23; cf. 1 Cor 1:14)

IV. Chronology of the Relationship of Paul, Timothy, and Titus with the Corinthian Church

The following chart is reproduced from pp. 101–3 of my NIGTC commentary of 2 Corinthians and is used with permission.

	Events	References	Date
1.	At the end of his "second missionary journey," after arrival from Athens, Paul spends eighteen months at Corinth.	Acts 18:1–8	Fall 50— Spring 52
2.	During that time Silas and Timothy arrive from Macedonia.	Acts 18:5	
3.	Paul has his hearing before Gallio.	Acts 18:12–17	Summer or Fall 51
4.	Paul proceeds from Corinth to Ephesus, where Aquila and Priscilla remain.	Acts 18:18–19	Spring 52
5.	During Paul's absence in Judea, Syria, Galatic Lycaonia, and Phrygia and for an indefinite time thereafter, Apollos preaches in Ephesus and Corinth before returning to Ephesus.	Acts 18:22–23; 18:24–19:1; 1 Cor 1:12; 3:4–6; 16:12	Spring— Summer 52
6.	Paul resides in Ephesus.	Acts 19:1–20:1	Fall 52— Spring 56
7.	Paul dispatches the "previous letter" (not extant and bearer unknown).	1 Cor 5:9–11	
8.	Timothy is sent to Macedonia (to initiate the collection?) and Corinth.	Acts 19:22; 1 Cor 4:19; 16:10	Early 55
9.	Paul receives news of bickering and cliques at Corinth from Chloe's people, and rebukes the Corinthian partisan spirit in 1 Cor 1–4.	1 Cor 1:11	

10.	An official delegation (Stephanas, Fortunatus, and Achaicus) arrives from Corinth with a letter (to which Paul replies in 1 Cor 7–16), confirms the report of Chloe's people, and conveys further disquieting news about immorality and litigiousness in the church (which Paul reproves in 1 Cor 5–6).	1 Cor 16:17; 7:1a; 11:18	
11.	1 Corinthians is delivered to Corinth, presumably by the three-man delegation.	1 Cor 16:12a	Spring 55
12.	Titus visits Corinth to initiate the collection by implementing the directions of 1 Cor 16:2.	2 Cor 8:6a	
13.	In spite of Paul's letter and the efforts of Timothy and Titus, and possibly because of the advent of Judaizing intruders from Palestine, conditions in the church at Corinth deteriorate, necessitating Paul's "painful visit" (Ephesus—Corinth—Ephesus).	2 Cor 11:4, 22; 2:1; 12:21; 13:2	Summer or Fall 55
14.	At some time after this visit, Paul (or his representative) is openly insulted at Corinth by a spokesman of an anti-Pauline faction.	2 Cor 2:5–8, 10; 7:12	
15.	Titus is sent from Ephesus to Corinth with the "severe letter" (not extant), with instructions to promote the collection if the letter proves successful and to meet Paul in Troas, or, failing that, in Macedonia (= Philippi).	2 Cor 2:3–4, 6, 9; 7:8, 12; 2:12–13; 7:5–6	Spring 56
16.	Paul leaves Ephesus shortly after the Demetrius riot, begins evangelism in Troas, but then suffers his "affliction in Asia."	Acts 19:23–20:1; 2 Cor 2:12–13; 1:8–11	Spring 56
17.	Paul travels on to Macedonia and engages in pastoral activity while organizing the collection in the Macedonian churches and awaiting the arrival of Titus from Corinth.	2 Cor 2:13; 7:5; Acts 20:2; 2 Cor 8:1–4; 9:2	Spring–Summer 56

18.	Titus arrives in Macedonia (? = Thessalonica or Berea) from Corinth with his welcome report of the Corinthians' responsiveness to the "severe letter."	2 Cor 7:5–16	Summer 56
19.	Paul begins to write 2 Cor 1–9 as he undertakes further pastoral and evangelistic work in Macedonia and probably in Illyricum.	Rom. 15:19–21	
20.	Meanwhile, the foreign agitators in Corinth continue to undermine Paul's authority there.	2 Cor 10–13	
21.	On returning to Macedonia and hearing of fresh problems at Corinth, Paul pens 2 Cor 10–13 and sends the whole letter to Corinth with Titus and his two colleagues.	2 Cor 8:17–18, 22	Fall 56
22.	Paul spends three months in Greece (= primarily Corinth) during which he writes Romans.	Acts 20:2b–3a; Rom. 15:25–28; 16:23 (cf. 1 Cor 1:14)	Winter 56–57, early 57
23.	Paul departs for Jerusalem, accompanied by delegates of the churches, in order to deliver the "collection for the poor."	Acts 20:3b–4; 21:17; 24:17	Spring 57

V. 1 Corinthians

A. *Its Occasion, Purpose, and Outcome*

What prompted Paul to begin dictating this letter to an amanuensis? (1) Disturbing news about the church had reached him from several of "Chloe's people," who were probably her business agents who represented her Ephesian interests in Corinth and traveled regularly between the two cities. They reported discord and splits within the church (1:11–12). (2) A letter had arrived from the church, presumably delivered by their three delegates, Stephanas, Fortunatus, and Achaicus who were with Paul at the time of writing (16:17), seeking Paul's pastoral advice on a range of pressing issues—marriage and celibacy (7:1, 25), food offered to idols (8:1), gifts of the Holy Spirit (12:1), the collection for the poor in the Jerusalem church 16:1), and the travel plans of Apollos (16:12). (3) From these three delegates, or another reliable source, Paul learned about immorality and lawsuits among church members (5:1–6:20).

Correspondingly, Paul's purposes in writing 1 Corinthians would have been threefold:

(i) to reply to the Corinthians' letter to him (chapters 7–16);

(ii) to express his consternation over the splits within the church (chapter 1–4), the blatant immorality (5:1–13; 6:12–20), and the litigation (6:1–11);

(iii) to indicate the travel plans of Apollos (16:12) and himself (16:5–9).

From Paul's statement, "I will stay on at Ephesus until Pentecost" (16:8), we learn both the place of writing (Ephesus) and the time of year (Fall). Luke's account of Paul's Ephesian ministry is recorded in Acts 19:1—20:1 and Paul's own summary is found in Acts 20:17–35. His daily schedule during this period seems to have been as follows:

(i) tent-making/leather work in the early morning to support himself and others (Acts 20:34);

(ii) disputing in the lecture hall of Tyrannus from 11 a.m. to 4 p.m. (so the Western text of Acts) (Acts 19:9);

(iii) visitation to fellow believers in their homes (Acts 20:20), both "night and day" (Acts 20:31).

At this time he faced vigorous opposition—"I fought wild beasts (= violent human opposition) in Ephesus" (15:32), and "there are many adversaries" (16:9).

The letter was written probably at the time represented by Acts 19:20 ("the word of the Lord spread widely and grew in power"). The reference to "two years" in Acts 19:10 would be Fall AD 52—Summer AD 54, so 1 Corinthians (Spring AD 55) would be later, but it would have been written before Acts 19:21, since this latter verse indicates Paul's intention to go to Jerusalem with "the collection for the poor," whereas in 1 Cor 16:3–4 he is uncertain about traveling to Jerusalem with the offering.

Any effort to trace the outcome of 1 Corinthians during the Summer and Fall of AD 55 is conjectural. 2 Cor 8:6a suggests that Titus may have visited at this time to initiate the collection for Jerusalem by implementing the directions of 1 Cor 16:2. But there may have been disagreement at Corinth about whether or not to follow Paul's instructions concerning the man guilty of incest (1 Cor 5:1–2, 7, 13), and if the interlopers from Judea arrived at this time with their Judaizing program, their relentless boasting (2 Cor 11:18–21), their false gospel (2 Cor 11:4) and their desire to discredit Paul (10:10–11), the situation in the church would have deteriorated dramatically (2 Cor 12:21), ultimately forcing Paul to pay his "painful visit" (see II. B. above).

B. *Basic Outlines*

Apart from the Introduction (1 Cor 1:1–9) and the Conclusion (1 Cor 16:1–24), Paul identifies five areas of concern in the church at Corinth:

1. Division (1:10—4:21)

2. Ethics (5:1—6:20)

3. Lifestyle (7:1—11:1)

4. Worship (11:2—14:40)

5. Eschatology (15:1–58)

Another way of outlining this letter is by the sources of Paul's information.

1. Chapters 1–4—an oral report from Chloe's people (1:11) regarding bickering, cliques, and the partisan spirit in the church.

2. Chapters 5–6—an oral report given by the church's deputies, Stephanas, Fortunatus, and Achaicus (16:7), regarding immorality and lawsuits.

3. Chapters 7–16—questions to Paul contained in a letter brought by these three men (7:1, 25; 8:1; 12:1; 16:1, 12).

C. *Outline of Content by Paragraph,* reflecting exegetical decisions reached on controversial points

(A) Greeting and Thanksgiving (1:1–9)

1:1–9

Paul identifies his addressees as "the (universal) church of God as it is found in Corinth," along with everyone everywhere who calls on the person of Christ for salvation. He thanks God for the evidence of his grace in the lives of the Corinthians as they exhibit varied spiritual gifts and enjoy fellowship with Christ during their wait for his return.

(B) Division (1:10–4:21)

(i) Splits over Preferred Leaders (1:10–17)

(ii) Christ Crucified as God's Power and Wisdom (1:18—2:5)

(iii) God's Wisdom Revealed by the Spirit (2:6–16)

(iv) The Roles of Church Leaders (3:1–23)

(v) The Apostles as Humble Stewards (4:1–13)

(vi) Paul's Fatherly Appeal and Warning (4:14–21)

1:10–17

Having been informed by some of Chloe's business agents of quarrelling in the church at Corinth, Paul appeals to the church members to be knitted together with the same outlook (1:10–11). They were aligning themselves with Paul or Apollos or Cephas or (perhaps in frustration) with Christ (1:12). These cliques may have arisen not only from preferences for certain leaders but also from rivalry between household groups. Paul asks, "Has Christ been divided up and apportioned out? Only Christ was crucified for you and baptisms took place only in his name!" In any case, Paul's main role was to preach the Good News about the cross of Christ, not to baptize (1:13–17).

1:18–25

This message about Christ's cross, about Christ crucified, has always been foolishness to self-styled scholars or philosophers who with all their worldly wisdom never gained a knowledge of God and are perishing (1:18–21). Although this crucified Messiah is an affront to Jews and complete nonsense to Gentiles (1:22–23), in the eyes of all believers, whether Jews or Greeks, he is God's demonstrated power and God's embodied wisdom (1:21, 24). In reality, God's "foolishness" is wiser than human wisdom, and God's "weakness" is stronger than human strength (1:25).

1:26–31

Paul continues his theme of God's reversal of human standards and expectations. Not many of the Corinthians were "wise" or influential or of noble birth (1:26), but what is significant is that God had chosen them—those whom the world despised as being powerless and insignificant nonentities. This was to render useless what the world considered well-established, so that no human could boast before God (1:27–29). God has made Christ to be the true wisdom for all those who are in Christ—a wisdom that brings righteousness, holiness and redemption (1:30). As Scripture says, "Let the person who boasts make his boast only about who the Lord is and what he has done" (1:31).

2:1–5

On his first visit Paul had refused to rely on eloquence or cleverness in his preaching which concentrated exclusively on Jesus as a crucified Messiah (2:1–2). Weak and timid as he was, his message had relied on the Spirit's powerful conviction, not any persuasive diction, so that the Corinthians' faith could focus on God's power, not on cleverness (2:3–5).

2:6–10a

For the spiritually mature Paul declared a message about God's secret wisdom that was foreign to the rulers of the present world order but was devised by God before time began for the ultimate glory of believers (2:6–7). This eternal divine plan of salvation for those who love God involved the crucifixion of Jesus Christ, the Lord of glory, and had now been disclosed to believers by God's Spirit (2:8–10a).

2:10b–16

It is God's Spirit, and he alone, who searches out everything, including the profound depths of God's thoughts and plans (2:10b–11). Having this Spirit, believers understand the blessings God has given to them and the apostles speak of these blessings in language taught by the Spirit (2:12–13). Those without the Spirit regard the truths that the Spirit imparts as sheer folly. But those who have God's Spirit have the discernment to evaluate everything and have actually gained access to the mind of Christ (2:14–16).

3:1–4

Because Paul's readers/hearers were not under the Spirit's sway, he had to feed them with infants' milk, not solid food (3:1–2). Proof of this immaturity was seen in their jealousy and quarrelling, as when someone says, "I look to Paul or Apollos as my leader!" (3:3–4).

3:5–9

As for Paul and Apollos, they are simply God's appointed servants, engaged in a single enterprise, one planting and the other watering the seed as fellow workmen who belong to God, the One who produces the all-important growth.

3:10–17

In the building at Corinth that God designed, Paul was like an expert master-builder who laid the only legitimate foundation, namely Jesus Christ (3:10–11). The materials anyone uses to build on that foundation will become apparent when fire tests the quality of each person's workmanship, leading to reward for some or the loss of reward for others if their work is burnt up—even if they themselves are just preserved (3:12–15). The church at Corinth was God's holy sanctuary, inhabited by the Spirit, a sanctuary that no one should destroy (3:16–17).

3:18–23

Since the world's wisdom is foolishness and totally futile in God's eyes, anyone who thinks they are wise should become a "fool" so that they may become truly wise (3:18–20). The Corinthians should stop boasting about Paul or Apollos or Cephas, for everything belongs to them—whether it be these men, or the world or life or death or the present or the future, and they belong to Christ just as Christ belongs to God (3:21–23).

4:1–5

As God's stewards, Apollos and Paul have been entrusted with the task of faithfully declaring God's secret purposes (4:1–2). Since it is the Lord who will finally assess Paul's stewardship, any assessment by his converts or any human court was of little consequence (4:3–4). In the Lord's assessment dark secrets and hidden motivations will be disclosed and appropriate commendation given to each person (4:5).

4:6–13

In speaking of God's crucial role in the ministry of Apollos and himself, Paul was highlighting the truth of the maxim, "Nothing beyond what is written" (= "Boast only in the Lord," 1:31), so that his readers would not make inflated claims about any of their leaders. All gifts had been received from God and should therefore not be a reason to boast (4:6–7).

To deflate the haughty conceit of the Corinthians, Paul indulges in sustained irony, comparing their imagined kingly reign with the actual humiliations of the apostolic band. It was as if God had put the apostles on public display as men doomed to die in the arena (4:8–9). The apostles are foolish, weak, and disgraced; the Corinthians are wise, strong, and honored (4:10). Then Paul itemizes apostolic privations, concluding that they had become the world's scum, the filthy scrapings off everyone's shoes (4:11–13).

4:14–21

With a dramatic change of tone, Paul now addresses his converts as their loving spiritual father, urging them to take him as their model to imitate (4:14–16). To this end he was sending Timothy to them to remind them of his Christian pattern of life (4:17). But he warns the arrogant members of the church that when he comes their fine talk will count for nothing. Would they prefer him to arrive rod in hand, or lovingly, in a gentle spirit (4:18–21)?

(C) Ethical Decisions (5:1–6:20)

    (i) Dealing with a Case of Incest (5:1–13)

    (ii) Litigation among Believers (6:1–11)

    (iii) Rejecting Sexual Immorality (6:12–20)

5:1–8

Paul chides the complacent Corinthians for their silent acceptance of a blatant case of sexual immorality in which a church adherent is in a sexual relationship with his widowed stepmother (5:1–2). Their course of action now should be to call a formal church meeting, knowing that the Lord Jesus and Paul are both spiritually present, and hand the man over to Satan for his body to be destroyed (5:3–5). They themselves should realize that even a little amount of leaven spreads through the whole batch of dough. By expelling the offender they would become like a fresh batch of dough and so celebrate the Christian Passover festival, using the unleavened bread of sincerity and truth (5:6–8).

5:9–13

Paul now corrects a misinterpretation of his earlier letter. When he told them not to associate with immoral people, it was a call not to withdraw from the world but rather to cut off all association with an immoral person known as a Christian (5:9–11). Discipline is appropriate only for those within the community of believers. In the present case, they must expel the wicked man from their community (5:12–13).

6:1–11

For believers to file lawsuits in pagan courts in front of unbelievers was totally inappropriate, given the fact that God's people themselves will one day judge the world and angels (6:1–3). Surely there must be people in the church wise enough to settle claims relating to everyday issues! (6:4–6). Having such lawsuits amounts to complete defeat. Better to put up with injustice or fraud—wrongs that the Corinthians themselves commit against their fellow believers (6:7–8). They must stop being deluded and remember that wrongdoers of all kinds, sexual or otherwise, have no share in the kingdom of God. Although the Corinthians once fell into that category, they had been cleansed and justified by the Lord Jesus Christ and the Spirit of God (6:9–11).

6:12–20

The Corinthian slogan, "everything is permissible," needs to be qualified, for not everything is helpful and one must not get enslaved by anything (6:12). God will destroy both food and the stomach, but that does not mean the body may be used in sexual immorality. It was made to honor the Lord, who himself was raised bodily from the dead just as believers will be (6:13–14). Since the bodies of believers form the limbs and organs of Christ and are one with him in the Spirit, how can a believer be also joined to a prostitute and become one body with her? (6:15–17). The person who engages in sexual immorality sins against their own body in a unique way, for the believer's body belongs to God by purchase and is a sanctuary for the Holy Spirit (6:18–20).

(D)   Lifestyle Issues (7:1—11:1)

(i) Principles of Marriage (7:1–16)

(ii) Concerning Change of Status (7:17–24)

(iii) Concerning the Unmarried and Widows (7:25–40)

(iv) Concerning Food Sacrificed to Idols (8:1–13)

(v) Paul's Rights and Self-Discipline as an Apostle (9:1–27)

(vi) Warnings from Israel's History (10:1–13)

(vii) Warning against Idolatry (10:14–22)

(viii) Christian Liberty (10:23—11:1)

Thus far in this letter Paul has addressed issues where his advice is clear-cut and unambiguous, often against the backdrop of his converts' unwarranted complacency. Now he turns to the two principal matters raised by the Corinthians in their letter to him, each introduced by "Now concerning" (*peri de*)—whether marriage was even legitimate for the believer (7:1), and whether the unmarried and widows should get married (7:25). In these cases Paul clearly indicates his preferences (7:6–7, 12, 25–26, 32, 35, 38, 40) in light of the current unspecified crisis (7:26a), without demanding compliance unless he knows of an unambiguous definitive saying of Jesus that settles the matter (7:10; cf. 7:12).

7:1–9

It seems that a group of proto-gnostic ascetics within the church of Corinth had tried to popularize a slogan, "It is good for a man not to have sexual relations with a woman." On the contrary, Paul replies, because of cases of immorality, faithful marital relations should be maintained, with both husband and wife giving their partner what is their due sexually, since neither has unlimited rights over their body (7:1–4). Any abstinence from sexual relations should perhaps be by mutual consent and for a limited period so as to avoid temptation to unfaithfulness (7:5). There was diversity of gift, but Paul's own preference for everybody was to stay unmarried, as he was (7:6–9).

7:10–16

The Lord's instruction is clear: a wife must not leave her husband, and a husband must not divorce his wife (7:10–11). In the case of mixed marriages, if the unbelieving partner consents to continue the marriage, there should be no divorce (7:12–13). This is because the unbeliever shares in their partner's consecration to God, just as their children share in that consecration (7:14). But if the unbelieving partner initiates a separation, the Christian brother or sister is not bound to their spouse. Even if they stay bound, there is no guarantee they will be the means of saving their partner (7:15–16).

7:17–24

Everyone should remain in the status they were in when God called them (7:17, 20, 24). The circumcised man should not seek to reverse his circumcision, and the uncircumcised man should not be circumcised, for in themselves circumcision and uncircumcision amount to nothing (7:18–20). Similarly, the slave, who is already the Lord's freed person. But if there is the chance to gain freedom, they should grasp it (7:21–22). Purchased at a great price, believers should not become slaves of human beings (7:23).

7:25–31

Regarding the unmarried, Paul's opinion, not the Lord's command, was that they should remain as they are, not seeking a change of status (7:25–27). However, to get married is not to sin, but those who do marry face special pressures (7:28). Since the appointed time is limited, those who are married, those who weep or rejoice, those who make purchases, and those who take advantage of this world's goods, should all remember that the world's structures are passing away (7:29–31).

7:32–40

The unmarried man or woman and the widow are preoccupied with the Lord's interests—how to please the Lord or be fully devoted to him (7:32, 34a). But the married man or woman is preoccupied with worldly affairs—how to please their partner, so their interests are divided (7:33, 34b). In saying this, Paul was encouraging undivided devotion to the Lord (7:35). If a man is concerned that he might not be acting honorably toward his betrothed virgin, let them marry; it is no sin and he is acting properly (7:36, 38a). But the man who has resolved to maintain the virginity of his betrothed and refrain from marriage is acting in an even more commendable way (7:37, 38b). A widow is free to marry anyone she wishes, provided it is a Christian marriage, but she would be happier to remain unmarried (7:39-40).

8:1-6

With regard to the question of the meat of animals that have been offered to pagan gods, some claim that "all of us have knowledge about this matter." But such knowledge produces self-conceit, whereas the person who loves God has been first chosen by him and so builds others up by love (8:1-3). It is true that an idol has no real existence and that there is no God but One. There may be many so-called "gods" and "lords," but for believers there is only one God, the Father, the source and goal of all, and one Lord, Jesus Christ, through whom everything came into existence (8:4-6).

8:7-13

But those who lack true knowledge and think of an idol as real, feel defiled in their conscience when they eat sacrificed meat. Eating this or that food does not alter one's standing with God but exercising one's liberty may be a stumbling block to those with sensitive consciences (8:7-9). If someone with a tender conscience sees another believer seated in an idol's temple, they may follow that example, violate their conscience, and have their faith destroyed. In causing a fellow believer to stumble, the person with a robust conscience is actually sinning against Christ (8:10-13).

9:1-12a

In defending his apostleship against the claim that he lacked apostolic credentials, Paul points to his vision of the resurrected Jesus and the very existence of a church at Corinth (9:1-3). His apostolic rights included hospitality, companionship of one's wife on ministry travel, and financial support (9:4-6). In justifying this latter principle of appropriate support for service rendered, he appeals to

the experience of soldiers, vineyard workers, shepherds, plough-
men, threshers, and even oxen treading out the grain while being
unmuzzled (9:7–10). Should not the sowing of a spiritual harvest
among the Corinthians merit a material harvest? (9:11–12a).

9:12b–18

Rather than availing himself of his rights, Paul chose to endure
hardship to avoid putting an obstacle in the gospel's way (9:12b,
15a). Those who perform temple duties or officiate at the altar also
are rewarded for their services, just as gospel preachers should
be (9:13–14). No one would ever deprive Paul of his ground for
boasting about financial independence. His strong compulsion to
continue preaching the gospel showed he had been entrusted with
a stewardship. His reward was to preach free of charge, foregoing
his rights (9:15–18).

9:19–23

Although Paul was not enslaved to anyone, he chose to become
everyone's slave in order to win as many people as possible over to
Christ (9:19). For the benefit of different categories of people, he
identified himself totally with them, in order to win them—Jews,
those subject to the law, those outside the Jewish law, and the weak
(9:20–22a). For the gospel's sake he became everything to everyone so that by all possible means he might bring salvation to some
(9:22b–23).

9:24–27

In the Isthmian Games only one competitor in a race wins the
prize, but all athletes must exercise self-discipline to win the
crown. Believers seek a crown that never fades (9:24–25).

   With an undistracted eye on the goal, Paul himself disciplined his body lest he be disqualified for the prize (9:26–27).

10:1–13

The Jewish spiritual ancestors of believers were sheltered under the pillar of cloud and passed safely through the Red Sea and so were baptized into fellowship with Moses (10:1–2). They all enjoyed the same spiritual food and water, yet God was displeased with most of them (10:3–5), for they craved what is evil and participated in idol worship and sexual orgy (10:6–7). As a result, some of them—in fact, a large number—met their deaths, some by snakes, others by the destroying angel (10:8–10). All this has been recorded for believers' instruction to prevent them from falling. But God is trustworthy and will provide deliverance for those under temptation or testing (10:11–13).

10:14–22

Paul now appeals to his readers' good sense as he associates idolatry that must be resolutely avoided with the issue of eating meat that has been sacrificed to idols—both involve communal participation. In the celebration of the Lord's Supper, the cup of wine and the broken bread point to a common participation in the body and blood of Christ: one loaf, one body (10:14–17). Similarly, when Israelites eat animal sacrifices they are corporate participants in the altar of sacrifice (10:18).

What does this mean? Not that an idol has real existence, but that pagan festal sacrifices are offered to demons, and believers cannot eat from the Lord's table and from the table of demons at the same time. The Lord is jealous! (10:19–22).

10:23–30

Some have a slogan, "I have liberty to do anything." But not everything is beneficial and builds people up (10:23–24). It is permissible to eat whatever is sold in the meat market. If a believer has accepted an invitation to an unbeliever's house for a meal, they should eat whatever food is provided—unless they are informed by someone (presumably a fellow believer) that the food had been offered in a temple sacrifice; that would offend that person's conscience (10:25–28). Freedom is properly shown by meeting the needs of others, even those with a weak conscience, the primary consideration (10:29–30).

10:31—11:1

Everything should be carried out to increase God's glory, avoiding giving offense to unbelievers or believers (10:31–32). Paul encourages his converts to follow his example, and Christ's, in trying to please everyone in every way, with a view to their salvation (10:33—11:1).

(E) Worship (11:2—14:40)

    (i) Instructions about Head Coverings in Worship (11:2–16)

    (ii) Correcting an Abuse of the Lord's Supper (11:17–34)

    (iii) Diversity of Spiritual Gifts (12:1–11)

    (iv) Unity and Diversity in the Body (12:12–31a)

    (v) Love, the Superior Way (12:31b—13:13)

    (vi) Tongues and Prophecy (14:1–25)

    (vii) Good Order in Church Meetings (14:26–40)

11:2–10

Paul applauds the Corinthians for adhering to Christian traditions (11:2). In particular, recognition of headship is crucial. A man should not pray or prophesy in public with his head covered by a veil, but a woman doing this should be veiled, otherwise it would be the same as having her hair shaved off, which would be a disgrace (11:3–6). A man should not be veiled since he reflects God's glory, just as a woman reflects man's glory. The first woman came from man and was created for man's sake. That is why a woman should be veiled as a sign of her authority to participate in worship publicly (11:7–10).

11:11–16

Men and women are interdependent, as at the beginning, although God is the source of everything (11:11–12). Nature teaches that long hair is a woman's glory; it was given to her as a head covering. So she ought to be veiled when leading in prayer (11:13–15). All of this is universal church custom (11:16).

11:17–22

But more harm than good resulted when the Corinthians gathered together, for there were divisive cliques among them and so there was no proper celebration of the Lord's Supper (11:17–20). In the general meal there was no sharing so that some got drunk while others went hungry and were humiliated for being poor. This was shameful in the church of God (11:21–22).

11:23–26

The tradition Paul had received he had passed on. It was that Jesus had broken some bread and said, "This represents my body. Do this as a way of remembering me." He also took a cup of wine, "This cup represents the new covenant, sealed by my blood"

(11:23–25). Whenever believers eat and drink these emblems, they are proclaiming the Lord's death until he returns (11:26).

11:27–34

To avoid profaning the body and blood of the Lord, people should first examine their motives, lest they bring judgment on themselves by failing to recognize the Lord's body symbolized by the bread and also his corporate Body (11:27–29). That is why some have experienced the Lord's discipline of poor health or even death, so as not to be condemned with the world (11:30–32). So when they gather, they should wait for one another; anyone hungry should eat at home. Further directions would be given when Paul arrived (11:33–34).

12:1–3

Regarding spiritual gifts, the Corinthians should remember that they once worshiped false gods that could not speak. Now the Spirit of God directs believers to say, "Jesus is Lord," but never "Jesus be cursed."

12:4–11

There are varieties of spiritual gifts and different types of service and activity, but it is one and the same Spirit or Lord or God behind them all, and the goal is always the common good (12:4–7). One and the same Spirit apportions his gifts to each believer individually as he alone chooses—gifts relating to counsel, knowledge, faith, healing, miracles, prophesying, insight, tongues, or interpretation (12:8–11).

12:12–31a

Although the human body has many different limbs and organs, it is a single body—as is the Body of Christ. Believers were all baptized in the one Spirit to form one Body, whether Jew or Gentile, slave or free (12:12–14). Many organs, but a single body, and each organ is an essential part of the body, be it a foot or a hand, an ear or an eye, the power of hearing or the sense of smell, the eye and the hand, the head and the feet (12:15–21). In fact, the parts that seem more feeble are actually indispensable and God has given greater honor to the less honorable parts that naturally lack dignity and so feel inferior. His aim was that all parts of the body should have equal concern for each other, so that both suffering and honor was shared (12:22–26).

Each believer is a part of the Body of Christ. God has appointed various people to perform different roles—apostles, prophets, teachers, those with the gift of performing miracles, or the gift of healing or helping others or leadership or speaking in tongues. There is diversity of gift—not all are apostles, for example. Believers should eagerly desire the gifts that are of the greatest value (12:27–31a).

12:31b–13:13

Here is the very best path to follow (12:31b)–the superior way of love.

13:1–3

Having fluency in languages or the gift of prophecy or profound knowledge or strong faith amounts to nothing if a person lacks love (13:1–2). Even if someone gives all their possessions to the poor or submits to severe persecution but has no love, their acts count for nothing (13:3).

13:4–13

Love is patient, kind, free of jealousy, boasting and pride. It never acts dishonorably, is not self-seeking or irritable, keeps no record of wrongs, but rejoices when truth triumphs. Love bears up, trusts, remains hopeful and steadfast right to the end (13:4–7). Prophesies, tongues and knowledge will one day be irrelevant, for when perfection arrives, what is partial will disappear, just as childish ways are abandoned in adulthood. At present vision is indistinct and knowledge is partial, but perfect clarity and full knowledge will come. For now there is faith, hope and love, with love the greatest (13:8–13).

14:1–5

Believers should desire the gifts given by the Spirit, especially prophecy, for whereas speaking in a tongue involves communicating with God, not others, and brings only personal benefit, prophesying is directed to other people, bringing them spiritual profit and building up the whole church. So prophesying is more important and is to be preferred over speaking in tongues. Only if tongues are interpreted is the whole community edified.

14:6–12

Spiritual benefit comes only if you are brought an unambiguous message such as a prophecy or a word of instruction. Unless the flute or lyre distinguishes between sounds, no one will recognize the tune. Or if the trumpet produces an ambiguous sound, no one will prepare for battle (14:8). An unintelligible message is pointless. In the case of languages, not to grasp the speaker's meaning makes both speaker and hearer foreigners. So seek the Spirit's gifts that build up the whole church (14:9–12).

14:13–19

The person who speaks in a tongue should pray for the ability to interpret it. Then they will pray and sing with their spirit, but also pray and sing using words they understand (14:13–15). If someone is praising God in an uninterpreted tongue, how can an enquirer say "Amen" at the end of a prayer? No one else is edified. Paul declares that in a church setting he would rather speak five understood words than ten thousand words in a tongue.

14:20–25

On this matter of speaking in tongues, Paul encourages the Corinthians to be adults, not childish. For stubborn unbelievers, like the Israelites of old, who refuse to listen to God, speaking in tongues is a judgmental sign, just as prophecy is designed for believers (14:20–22). Enquirers who enter the church meeting during tongue speaking will pronounce everyone crazy, but if they come during prophesying they will be convicted of sin as their secrets are exposed and they will worship God (14:23–25).

14:26–33a

As the church gathers, everything should be done for the benefit of all—whether it be a hymn, instruction, a revelation, a tongue, or an interpretation. Two or at the most three people could speak in tongues, but only if there is an interpretation (14:26–28). If two or three prophets speak, the rest should evaluate. If a revelation is received by someone, let the first speaker finish. Prophets should speak one by one, for prophets remain in control of their prophetic inspiration. God is a God of peace, not disorder! (14:29–33a).

14:33b–40

Women should remain silent; it is their role to be submissive. They should ask their husbands at home if they have questions. God's word (and church tradition) did not originate with the Corinthians! (14:33b–36). What Paul had been saying was a directive from the Lord that they should recognise. In sum, they should be eager to prophesy, not forbid speaking in tongues, and do everything in an orderly way (14:37–39).

(F) Eschatology (15:1–58)

    (i) The Resurrection of Christ (15:1–11)

    (ii) The Resurrection of the Dead (15:12–34)

    (iii) The Resurrection Body (15:35–58)

Verses 1–34 of 1 Cor 15 discuss the *that* of the resurrection (*hoti*, "that," vv. 4, 12), and verses 35–58 the *how* of the resurrection (*pōs*, "how," v. 35). Paul first enunciates the premise he shares with his opponents, namely, the resurrection of Christ (vv. 1–11), and then proceeds to draw a conclusion from this premise, namely, that the dead in Christ will rise (vv. 12–32). In this latter section, he shows the outcome of denying this conclusion, namely, the denial of the premise (vv. 12–19), and specifies the outcome of accepting this conclusion, namely, the function of Christ in the Last Days (vv. 20–28). Part two of the chapter (vv. 35–58) spells out two difficulties with the conclusion that the dead in Christ will rise: first, the nature of the resurrection body (vv. 35–50); secondly, the destiny of Christians alive at the second Advent (vv. 51–57).

15:1–11

Paul reminds the Corinthians of the essence and primary importance of the gospel that he had received and had passed on to them—the death of Christ in accordance with the Scriptures, his burial, his resurrection in accordance with the Scriptures, and his appearance to Cephas and then to the Twelve (15:1–5). Then followed further appearances, including one to Paul himself, the least of the apostles, one who had formerly persecuted the church. His apostolic role and his distinctive toil were a tribute to God's grace. He proclaimed the same message as the other apostles (15:6–11).

15:12–28

An influential sector of the church at Corinth evidently rejected the notion of resurrection (15:12b), conceding that Christ rose (cf. 15:12a) but perhaps arguing that only the immortal soul survives death or that the resurrection is past since at baptism believers were raised with Christ. The futurity and the bodily nature of the resurrection were being denied.

Working from the agreed premise, Paul argues that the resurrection of the dead stands or falls with the resurrection of Christ, and that if Christ was not raised the gospel message is hollow, believers' faith is futile, and deceased believers are lost (15:12–19). Just as death entered the world because of Adam and all humans now die, so the resurrection of the dead came about because of Christ, the firstfruits of the full harvest of believers (15:20–23). After Christ's second coming the End will arrive, when God will vanquish all his enemies including death and place them under Christ's feet, and Christ will surrender the kingdom to his Father and place himself under God's authority, so that God may be totally supreme (15:24–28).

15:29–34

To consolidate his argument, Paul adds two *ad hominem* points: the practice of some to be baptized for the dead (15:29), and the pointlessness of constant apostolic peril and danger if there is no resurrection (15:30–32). Then he adds a warning to avoid bad company and sinful conduct (15:33–34).

15:35–41

Here Paul is establishing the possibility of a form of human embodiment different from the present human body. One sews a bare grain as a seed, not the final plant. God provides it with a distinctive "body" of his choosing. There are various forms of "flesh" for humans, beasts, birds and fish, just as there are both heavenly and earthly bodies with different types of splendor.

15:42–58

It will be similar for the resurrection of the dead. The sowing of the earthly body is marked by decay, dishonor, and weakness; the rising is marked by immortality, splendor, and power. An earthly body is sown, a spiritual body is raised (15:42–44). The first human being, Adam, was created from the earth's dust and became a living soul; but the last Adam has a heavenly origin and is a life-giving Spirit. Humans are like the first man; believers will be like the heavenly Man (15:45–49).

Physical bodies cannot inherit the kingdom of God. Here is a mystery: Not all believers will die, but all, whether dead or alive, will suddenly be transformed and become immortal. When the perishable mortal body puts on an imperishable immortal body, Scripture will be fulfilled that says, "Death has been swallowed up in victory." Victory over death's sting comes through Jesus Christ.

The Corinthians should therefore devote their full energy to the work of the Lord (15:50–58).

(G) Conclusion (16:1–24)

(i) The Collection for the Jerusalem Church (16:1–4)

(ii) Personal Requests (16:5–18)

(iii) Final Greetings (16:19–24)

16:1–4

Paul gives his directions for the collection. The believers are to set aside their contributions regularly and choose their delegates who will accompany him to Jerusalem if it is advisable for him to go.

16:5–18

Paul was planning to stay on in Ephesus where there was opportunity for effective ministry in spite of many opponents, and then to visit the Corinthians for a while if the Lord permitted, so they could equip him for his travel. When Timothy arrives, he should be treated with appreciation for his service, not shown contempt. They should send him back to Paul in peace. Apollos would visit them when there was good opportunity (16:5–12). They themselves were to stand firm in their faith and do everything in love. They should submit to people like Stephanas, who with Fortunatus and Achaicus refreshed Paul's spirit and made up for the Corinthians' absence by giving him help (16:13–18).

16:19–24

Paul sends greetings from the churches of Asia, including the brothers and sisters in Ephesus, from Aquila and Prisca and their house church, and from himself along with his love.

VI. 2 Corinthians

A. *Its Occasion, Purpose, and Outcome*

The circumstances that prompted Paul to send 2 Corinthians were twofold: the arrival of his pastoral assistant Titus, who brought welcome news of the favorable response of the majority of the Corinthians to the "severe letter" (see III. C. above) (2 Cor 7:6–16), and the arrival of fresh, disturbing news about the situation at Corinth (reflected in 2 Cor 10–13). Its destination was not only "the church of God in Corinth" but also "all God's holy people throughout Achaia" (2 Cor 1:1) in places such as Athens (see Acts 17:34) and Cenchreae (see Rom 16:1). It may be dated in the Fall of AD 56, some eighteen months after 1 Corinthians (Spring AD 55). Several references within 2 Corinthians suggest that Paul was in the province of Macedonia when writing (7:5; 8:1; 9:2–4; cf. Acts 20:1–2). Of special significance is the present tense (*kauchōmai*) in 9:2, "I have been boasting about it (your eagerness to help) to the Macedonians." This provenance is confirmed by those Greek manuscripts which note, in the subscription to the letter, that it was written "from Philippi."

The apostle's *overall* purpose in writing was to promote his converts' upbuilding (12:19; cf. 10:8; 13:10), and in particular their restoration (13:9) to proper relations with God, with himself, and with one another. Paul's *specific* purposes were (1) to express his great relief and delight at the Corinthians' positive response to his "severe letter" that had been delivered and reinforced by Titus (2:6, 9, 12–14; 7:5–16); (2) to exhort the Corinthians to complete their promised collection for the believers at Jerusalem before his arrival on the next visit (8:6–7, 10–11; 9:3–5); (3) to prepare them for his forthcoming, hopefully mutually advantageous, visit by having them engage in self-examination and self-judgment (12:14; 13:1, 5, 11) so that they could discover the proper criteria for distinguishing between rival apostolates (10:7, 14–15; 11:2, 5–6; 12:11–12; 13:6–7, 10) and so that Paul could be spared the pain of having to exercise discipline (10:2, 5–6, 11; 12:19–21; 13:10).

Regarding the letter's outcome, see above II. C., The Final Visit (Acts 20:2–3).

B. *Basic Outlines*

The epistle falls into three clearly defined sections.

1. Chapters 1–7	Paul's Explanation of his Conduct and Apostolic Ministry Theme: "comfort in the midst of affliction" (1:3–7; 7:4, 7, 13) Tone: "I must rejoice" (2:3; 6:10; 7:4, 7, 9, 13, 16) Dominant emphasis: apologetic
2. Chapters 8–9	Paul's Summons to Complete the Collection Theme: "generosity in the midst of need" (8:2, 9; 9:5–6, 11–13) Tone: "You must finish (your collection)" (8:6, 11; 9:3, 5) Dominant emphasis: exhortatory
3. Chapters 10–13	Paul's Defense of his Apostolic Authority Theme: "strength in the midst of weakness" (11:30; 12:9–10; 13:9) Tone: "I must boast" (11:16–18, 21, 30; 12:1, 5–6, 9) Dominant emphasis: polemical

C. *Outline of Content by Paragraph*, reflecting exegetical decisions reached on controversial points

Paul's Explanation of his Conduct and Apostolic Ministry
(2 Cor 1–7)

(A) Introduction (1:1–11)

    (i) Salutation (1:1–2)

    (ii) A Doxology Celebrating Divine Comfort (1:3–7)

    (iii) Deliverance from a Deadly Peril (1:8–11)

1:1–2

In his customary salutation Paul combines and modifies the traditional Greek and Hebrew greetings: *chairein* ("greetings!" becomes *charis* ("grace") and *šālôm* becomes *eirēnē*, both meaning "peace." Grace and peace come jointly from the Father and the Son.

1:3–7

Paul ascribes praise to God for his constant encouragement in the midst of a variety of distressing circumstances which he identifies as "Christ's sufferings." The purpose of his ongoing experience of divine comfort was to equip him to be an agent of God's bountiful comfort and encouragement to those facing any kind of distress—including the Corinthians.

1:8–11

After the salutation Paul normally expresses thanksgiving for his readers and records his prayer requests for them, but here he is preoccupied with his own situation as he gives thanks to God for his recent deliverance from a devastating affliction in Asia that brought him face to face with death—and that threatened to recur. This radical departure from his literary custom indicates how overwhelming and debilitating this confrontation with death must have been. So he now solicits his readers' prayer for himself (1:11)!

Elsewhere Paul could say "not a day but I am at death's door" (1 Cor 15:31, Moffatt) and "I have been exposed to death again and again" (2 Cor 11:23), but the present experience was unique: the Paul who confesses "nothing is beyond my power in the strength of him who makes me strong" (Phil 4:13, TCNT) now asserts that his affliction was "beyond measure, beyond our capability to cope with (*kath'* hyper*bolēn* hyper *dynamin*), so that we were forced to abandon even any hope of survival" (2 Cor 1:8). His deliverance was a veritable resurrection (2 Cor 1:9). Various identifications of this affliction have been proposed—opposition to Paul at Ephesus, his suffering of "the thirty-nine stripes" (2 Cor 11:24), imprisonment, the Demetrius riot (Acts 19:23–41; but most probably it was a prostrating attack of a recurrent malady that he later identifies as a "thorn in my flesh" (2 Cor 12:7). It was this death-threatening experience in Asia that lay behind his theology of death in 2 Cor 5:1–10.

(B) Paul's Conduct Defended (1:12–2:13)

   (i) Characteristics of his Conduct (1:12–14)

   (ii) Charge of Fickleness Answered (1:15–22)

   (iii) A Canceled Painful Visit (1:23—2:4)

   (iv) Forgiveness for the Offender (2:5–11)

   (v) Restlessness at Troas (2:12–13)

1:12—2:4

Paul faced a series of accusations from certain nameless people in the congregation—that he had behaved deviously and insincerely towards the church; that his written communications were surreptitious in their intent and execution; that he vacillated in his travel plans; and that he adopted a domineering attitude toward his converts (1:12–13, 17, 24). We can reconstruct these charges against Paul by examining his response: he had always acted with integrity and godly sincerity (1:12); his letters were unambiguous, without a hidden meaning (1:13); yes, he had altered his travel plans, but the change was designed to avoid another painful visit—he was not a "Yes–No" man (1:15–19) who lorded it over his Corinthian friends, but rather a loving sensitive friend who avoided causing them grief (1:23–2:4).

2:5–11

"The majority" (2 Cor 2:6) of the Corinthians had followed Paul's instructions in his "severe letter" and had penalized the nameless offender in some unknown way (see III. C. above). But to prevent this repentant believer from being engulfed by excessive remorse and the whole church falling into a Satanic trap, Paul now counsels them to forgive the offender and reinstate him within the community. The implied minority may have been a pro-Pauline group of "ultra-Paulinists" who advocated a continuation or increase of the punishment already inflicted by the majority.

2:12–13

In a stark confession of his restlessness (2:12–13), Paul indicates that he curtailed evangelistic opportunity at Troas and set off for Macedonia. This deep unease was prompted by his persistent uncertainty about the success of his "severe letter" at Corinth and by the ominous failure of Titus to arrive at Troas as arranged.

(C) Major Digression—The Apostolic Ministry Described
(2:14–7:4)

(i) The Grandeur and Superiority of the Apostolic Ministry
   (2:14—4:6),

(ii) The Suffering and Glory of the Apostolic Ministry
   (4:7—5:10)

(iii) The Essence and Exercise of the Apostolic Ministry
   (5:11—6:10)

(iv) The Openness and Consolation of the Apostolic Ministry
   (6:11—7:4)

2:14–17

2 Corinthians 2:14—7:4 is the longest digression in all of Paul's letters. With its reference to Paul's arrival in Macedonia, 7:5 clearly resumes 2:13 that spoke of his departure from Macedonia. Because of Titus's safe arrival in Macedonia with a positive report of the Corinthian reaction to the "severe letter" described in 7:5–16, Paul breaks into a brief doxology (2:14) at the thought of that joyful reunion with Titus. In recent happy events the apostle perceived God's vindication of his apostleship, not only in Corinth but "in every place." Using the imagery of the Roman "triumph" with its victory procession, he pictures himself and his fellow apostles as (paradoxically) prisoners of war, willing and joyful captives in God's triumphal pageant. It is through them that God diffuses the sweet aroma which is the knowledge of Christ (2:14). So far from being fraudulent hucksters, the apostles deliver their message as those commissioned by God and accountable to him (2:17b).

3:1–6

Two further issues about Paul's actions (see 1:12–17 for the earlier ones) were apparently raised by some at Corinth. Perhaps in the view of certain intruders who were making a profit out of preaching (2:17a), Paul was flaunting his credentials (3:1a) and had failed to produce letters of recommendation from Jerusalem (3:1b). This second objection he answers by observing that the Corinthians themselves were his living commendatory letter, composed by Christ and transcribed by himself (3:2–3). As for the matter of credentials, his competence to serve as God's agent to promulgate the new covenant came from God himself (3:4–6).

3:7–11

Paul establishes the superiority of the apostolic ministry by pointing to the surpassing glory of the new covenant. Alluding to the circumstances surrounding the formation of the old covenant (Exod 34:29–35), he argues that if the old dispensation that brought death and condemns people was accompanied by dazzling glory, the new dispensation that provides a right standing before God and is destined to last forever must be correspondingly more glorious and even totally eclipses the former glory.

3:12–18

Paul suggests that Moses veiled the dazzling radiance of his face not only to prevent the Israelites from gazing in stunned amazement but also to demonstrate that the glory of the Sinai covenant would be eclipsed. To the present day the same veil covers the hearts of the Jews during the reading of the old covenant as they fail to recognize the impermanence of that covenant. Only when they come to be in the Messiah (3:14) or turn to the Lord (3:16) is the veil set aside. Then freedom from the veil of ignorance is gained and there begins a progressive transformation of believers into the glorious likeness of the Lord Christ.

4:1-6

Once more Paul is compelled to address malicious criticism aris-ing within the congregation: that he espoused underhand and disgraceful tactics (cf. 1:13) and tampered with the Old Testament Scriptures and the gospel itself. He responds by appealing to his full disclosure of Christian truth that resonates with every human conscience and is undertaken with God as onlooker and ultimate judge (4:2). Then he applies the concept of veiling to all unbeliev-ers, not simply unbelieving Jews (as in 3:14–15). In the case of all those who are perishing, be they Jews or Gentiles, the god who rules over the present evil age has blinded their understanding, thus preventing the light of the gospel from shining into their hearts and dispelling the darkness—the gospel that displays the glory of Christ who is the visible and exact representation of God.

4:7-15

Paradoxes abound as Paul describes the realities of his apostolic service. First, the priceless treasure of the glorious gospel of Christ is contained in human earthenware jars that are fragile, unat-tractive and relatively worthless, so that the gospel's power may be clearly seen to derive from God alone (4:7). Then a quartet of paradoxes follows: "troubles press on us from every quarter, but we are not hemmed in and crushed; bewildered by circumstances, but never driven to despair; relentlessly persecuted by others but never abandoned by God; often knocked to the ground, but never permanently 'grounded'" (4:8–9). In spite on his experiencing constant exposure to perilous hazards and death, comparable to the "dying" that Jesus knew, he simultaneously displayed the resur-rection life of Jesus (4:10–11). Alongside this "life in the midst of death" was a faith that could not remain silent, given the prospect of sharing Jesus' resurrection (4:13–14).

4:16–18

Paul found splendid compensation for his relentless toil and suffering in the constant rejuvenation of his spiritual energy that matched the progressive weakening of his physical powers (4:16). In fact, the solid load of lasting glory being currently produced far outweighed his relatively insignificant and momentary afflictions (4:17). These afflictions seemed light and temporary because his gaze was fixed on unseen realities (4:17).

5:1–8

Paul realized that the traumatic encounter with death that he had recently experienced in Asia (1:8–9), totally disconcerting as it was, could recur (1:10), so he now reviews the threefold ground for the believer's confidence in God when facing death. The first source of divine comfort was the certainty of the future possession of a spiritual body, a replacement for his current tent-house that God would supply and would last forever in heaven (5:1). This new heavenly dwelling meant he would never experience disembodied nakedness. Rather, his mortal body would be swallowed up by immortality (5:2–4). Secondly, as a preparation for this ultimate transformation God has given believers his Spirit who is both a deposit and a pledge of what is to come (5:5). The third ground for confidence in every circumstance is knowing that at death faith gives place to sight as the believer takes up permanent residence in the immediate presence of Christ (5:6–8).

5:9–10

Paul's constant aim—in effect his life motto—was to be pleasing to Christ (5:9). This aim was wholly in keeping with his destiny of permanent residence with Christ (5:8) and his future accountability to

Christ who would evaluate his actions carried out during his life on earth (5:10).

5:11–15

Filled with reverential awe before Christ as his future judge, Paul tried to convince everyone of the messiahship and lordship of Jesus. Also he was attempting to persuade the Corinthians that his apostolic credentials and conduct were sound (5:11). He was providing them with an opportunity to champion his cause against his critics within the church who were preoccupied with externals and had accused him of being "out of his mind," perhaps because of his visionary experiences (cf. Acts 22:17–21) or his allegedly esoteric teaching (cf. Acts 26:24) (5:12–13). His compelling motivation for all his service was to follow the example of the love Christ showed in his death for everyone and to give Christ his total devotion (5:14–15).

5:16—6:2

Paul's own conversion marked the arrival of a new order of reality and a twofold alteration of attitude: no longer was Christ regarded as a misguided messianic pretender and no longer was the Jew–Gentile divide regulative in his thinking (5:16–17). This new act of creation was God's work who was in Christ, reconciling the world to himself, and who had entrusted the apostles with the task of announcing and applying this reconciliation as his mouthpiece and as Christ's ambassadors (5:18–20). In this era of God's gracious salvation, those who are reconciled have had their sins forgiven and have gained a permanently right relationship with God (5:19–6:2).

6:3–10

These verses contain (in 6:4b–10) one of four catalogs of hardships in 2 Corinthians (the others are 4:8–9; 11:23b–29; 12:10). So far from discrediting his ministry, his sufferings validated his role as God's servant (6:3–4a). The first segment of the catalog of wide-ranging apostolic experience deals with outward circumstances—general trials calling for steadfast endurance, sufferings inflicted by humans, and then self-inflicted austerity (6:4b–5). Then follows a list of inward character qualities (6:6), four items of spiritual equipment (6:7), and finally an itemized tabulation of the vicissitudes of Paul's ministry (6:8–10). This latter list outlines seven paradoxes of apostolic life (e.g., "poor and yet enriching many") that contrast the worldly and divine perspectives on Paul's life.

6:11–13

Rarely does Paul address his readers by name, but now with his emotions stirred as he reflects on his deep affection for the Corinthians and his total openness with them as his spiritual children, he pleads for the removal of any constriction in their relationship with him and for complete reciprocity of affection as a "fair exchange."

6:14—7:1

This is a minor digression, since 7:2a repeats 6:13 and 7:4 resumes 6:11. In this segment there are six exhortations that call for three actions: avoid mismatched unions (6:14), be separate from all that defiles (6:17; 7:1a), and pursue holiness (7:1b). Interspersed between these exhortations are seven promises—in essence, God will be present and active among them as their God, he will welcome them and be their Father (6:16–18)—that cite seven OT passages found in the Law and the Prophets of the Hebrew canon. Evidently some Corinthians had become defiled, perhaps by sharing meals at idol-shrines or by continuing to attend ceremonies in pagan temples.

7:2–4

Here Paul returns to the travel narrative that was suspended at 2:13. In spite of the accusations made against him, Paul boldly asserts that he had never wronged or ruined or defrauded anyone. On the contrary, his confidence and pride in the Corinthians was so unmistakable that his joy knew no bounds.

(D) Paul's Joy at the Corinthians' Repentance (7:5–16)

- (i) Comfort in Macedonia (7:5–7)
- (ii) The "Severe Letter" and the Joy and Affection of Titus (7:8–16)

7:5–7

Even after Paul arrived in Macedonia, conflict raged around him and anxiety reigned within. In the safe arrival of Titus with good news about Corinth, Paul traced God's comforting intervention.

7:8–16

The purpose, effect and identification of the "severe letter" have been discussed above (III. C.). The focus in these present verses is on the varied reactions of the Corinthians, Paul, and Titus to the receipt of this "severe letter" and its effects.

The Corinthians experienced a godly sorrow that prompted repentance (7:8–10), a zealous concern and eagerness to clear themselves from blame, indignation at the guilty party, alarm over their behavior, longing to see Paul in person, zeal to follow Paul's instructions, and resolve to see justice done (7:11–12, 15). At first Paul regretted having written the letter but his regret was short-lived as he learned of the Corinthians' repentance and obedience (7:8–9, 15). He had no reason to be embarrassed about his earlier boasting to Titus about them (7:14). He was encouraged (7:13) and completely confident of them (7:16). Titus felt joy and deep affection for them because they had received him with fear and trembling and had greatly refreshed his spirit by their obedience (7:13, 15).

Paul's Summons to Complete the Collection (2 Cor 8–9)

From the viewpoint of psychological tactics, there was no better platform from which to launch an appeal for financial action than to remind the Corinthians of their recent warm-hearted response to Titus and the "severe letter" and of his own complete confidence in them (7:6–16). The church certainly knew of this offering "for the poor among the Lord's people in Jerusalem" (Rom 15:26), for he had given them directions about the project in 1 Cor 16:1–4 in response to their own enquiry (implied by his "now concerning" in 1 Cor 16:1).

Although the church had agreed to contribute to the fund and had made a promising start (8:6, 10; 9:2), progress had apparently stalled for over a year (probably since Spring AD 55), owing to: (1) the disturbing events that occurred during Paul's "painful visit;" (2) the affair regarding "the offender" and its aftermath (2:5–11; 7:12) that would have adversely affected attitudes toward Paul; and (3) the negative influence of the intruders from Judea (see the discussion at 11:5) who received some monetary support from Corinthian sympathizers (11:5–12, 20). The essence of the apostle's call in 2 Cor 8–9 is "Now then, complete the work" (8:11) "and do so before I arrive" (9:3–5).

(A) The Need for Generosity (8:1–15)

   (i) The Generosity of the Macedonians (8:1–6)

   (ii) A Plea for Liberal Giving (8:7–12)

   (iii) The Aim of Equality (8:13–15)

8:1–6

With pastoral tact Paul begins with an example to follow, not an urgent plea. Writing from the province of Macedonia where he was currently visiting churches (9:2), he affirms that the rich generosity of the Macedonians was (paradoxically) the overflow of their boundless joy and rock-bottom poverty. He attributes this to God's grace (8:1–2). In giving beyond their resources and devoting themselves to Paul's project as well as to the Lord, they exceeded Paul's expectations, so that Titus's forthcoming visit to stimulate the completion of the Corinthian gift was appropriate (8:3–6).

8:7–12

As Paul encourages—not demands—generous giving, he appeals to the Corinthians' pursuit of spiritual excellence, the exemplary earnestness of the Macedonians, and the supreme example in Christ of eagerness and generosity in giving as a demonstration of love: if the Macedonians gave when they were desperately poor (8:2), Christ gave when he was immeasurably rich (8:7–9). Although the Corinthian need to complete the project was urgent, given their start about a year earlier, their contribution should be according to their means, not reckless (8:10–12).

8:13–15

One of the purposes of the collection project was to achieve equality in the supply of the necessities of life, an equality between the relatively prosperous Corinthians and the poor within the Jerusalem church. This was a divinely sanctioned goal, for during the wilderness journey of the Israelites God himself created comparable equality by miraculously equalizing the quantities of manna that each person had gathered (Exod 16:17–18). If that equality was enforced, the collection's desired equality is voluntary.

(B) The Mission of Titus and His Companions (8:16—9:5)

(i) The Delegates and Their Credentials (8:16–24)

(ii) The Need for Readiness (9:1–5)

At the beginning and end of 2 Cor 8–9 Paul focuses on the motives that should impel them to prompt action, describing first the need for generosity (8:1–15), then the results of such generosity (9:6–15). Nestled between these two sections is a passage (8:16–9:5) in which Paul indicates how he plans to facilitate the fulfillment of their intent (8:11; 9:2) and promise (9:5). He is about to dispatch a three-man delegation to Corinth (8:16–24), who, in advance of his own arrival, will oversee the completion of the collection, so that pressured giving can be avoided once he arrives (9:3–5).

8:16–24

In this virtual "letter of commendation" (cf. (3:1) from Paul to the church of Corinth, he first emphasizes that his deputy and fellow worker, Titus, will be visiting with much enthusiasm and on his own initiative (8:16–17). His two traveling colleagues are delegates of the Macedonian churches and an honor to Christ. These careful arrangements would ensure that Paul did what was right and honorable in human eyes as well as in God's eyes (cf. Prov 3:4), thereby guaranteeing the integrity of the process. All three men were to be treated with the appropriate respect and love (8:18–24).

9:1–5

Paul had boasted confidently to the Macedonians about the Corinthian "eagerness to help," their "readiness to give," and their general "enthusiasm" about the venture. Since this had stirred most of the Macedonians not only to begin but also to finish their contribution (9:2; cf. 8:1–5), now Paul could in turn use the Macedonian example to urge the Corinthians to finish (8:6–8), lest his boasting should prove to be unjustified if other Macedonians should arrive in Corinth only to discover the collection languishing there (9:3–4). The visit of the three brothers would ensure Paul was not humiliated this way and that the Corinthian donation would be a gift bringing blessing and not a gift reflecting avarice (9:5).

(C) *The Resources and Results of Generosity (9:6–15)*

    (i) God's Enrichment of the Giver (9:6–11)

    (ii) The Offering of Prayer to God (9:12–15)

9:6–11

In an extensive use of agricultural imagery, the believer who gives is viewed as both a sower and a reaper, what is given is the seed, and the outcome of the giving is the harvest. Scanty sowing results in a meager harvest, while plentiful sowing produces a bountiful harvest (9:6). The first benefit of lavish sowing is ongoing enrichment by God in both the material and the spiritual realms, an enrichment that aims to promote ongoing generosity by the cheerful giver (9:8–10). Generosity channeled through the relief fund Paul was administering would produce thanksgiving to God on the part of the recipients (9:11).

9:12–15

The second result of generous giving relates to the recipients of the Corinthians' gift—the Jerusalem poor in particular and the whole Jerusalem church in general. They would offer many prayers of gratitude to God for his superlative grace in the lives of the Corinthians that was shown in their generosity (9:12–13). Also they would intercede for their fellow believers in Corinth in prayers that expressed their affectionate longing for them (9:14). Appropriately, Paul concludes with an expression of thanks to God for his gift that is beyond description—the gift of the Messiah (9:15).

What do we know about the success of the collection in Corinth and in Jerusalem? About five months after he finished writing 2 Corinthians in Macedonia (Fall AD 56), Paul wrote to the Christians in Rome (early AD 57) while visiting Corinth in accordance with his stated plans (2 Cor 12:14; 13: 1–2; cf. Acts 20:2–3; Rom 16;23; 1 Cor 1:14) on what was to be his third and final visit to the city (see "The Final Visit," II. C. above). In Romans 15:26–27a he states that "Macedonia and Achaia have been pleased to make some contribution for the poor among God's people in Jerusalem. Yes, they were pleased to do so." "Achaia" here refers to the people in the churches of Achaia, including the Corinthians (cf. 2 Cor 9:2). Clearly, then, the believers at Corinth had heeded Paul's appeal and brought their contribution to completion.

As for the collection's success in Jerusalem, it was the Jerusalem leaders who "warmly welcomed" or "eagerly received" the Gentile delegation that delivered the offering (Acts 21:17). After Paul had given a report of his ministry among the Gentiles (presumably including reference to the successful collection), the Jerusalem church "praised God" (Acts 21:19-20).

Paul's motivation in promoting the offering was many-sided: to fulfill a promise of material aid (Gal 2:10); to express in a tangible way the interdependence of the members of the Body of Christ (1 Cor 12:25-26); to have Gentile believers dramatize in material terms their indebtedness to the mother church in Jerusalem (Rom 15:19, 27); to symbolize the unity of Jew and Gentile in Christ (Eph 2:11-22); and to win over those Jewish Christians who entertained suspicions about his Gentile mission (cf. Acts 11:2-3).[3]

Paul's Defense of His Apostolic Authority (2 Cor 10-13)

Anyone reading through 2 Corinthians will notice the sudden and dramatic change at 10:1-2 and beyond. Paul moves from the warm-hearted appeals of chapters 8-9 to a vigorous self-defense and polemic in chapters 10-13. Those scholars who regard 2 Cor 10-13 as the largest part of an earlier or a later letter to Corinth have no need to account for any change at 10:1—in these two explanations a totally different occasion and purpose is proposed for these four chapters.

Those who defend the integrity or unity of 2 Corinthians must suggest an adequate reason for the change of tone and style. It is the contention of the present writer[4] that chapters 1-9 were written in stages over a considerable period and that after Paul had written these chapters, he received distressing news of further problems at Corinth that prompted him to write chapters 10-13 and then send off all thirteen chapters as a single letter. What this news might have been can only be conjectured. We may suppose that the intruders from Judea (see the note at 2 Cor 11:5) had

3. See further Murray J. Harris, *The Second Epistle to the Corinthians: A Commentary on the Greek Text* (Grand Rapids: Eerdmans/Milton Keynes: Paternoster, 2005), 87-101.

4. Harris, *Second Epistle to the Corinthians*, 8-51, 104-5.

become more open and aggressive in their effort to discredit Paul and that the Corinthians in general had become more receptive to their teaching and more open to their influence. On this view 2 Cor 10–13 is Paul's response to more intense opposition at Corinth.

It should be said that the difference in tone and technique between chapters 1–9 and chapters 10–13 may be easily overdrawn, for there are elements of remonstrance in the earlier chapters (e.g., 2:17; 5:12; 6:14) and reassurances of warm affection in the last four chapters (e.g., 11:2; 12:14–15, 19). Moreover, the presence of apology, exhortation, and polemic can be traced in each of the three sections of the letter.[5]

Throughout these four chapters Paul often refers to a group of unnamed people, whether his adversaries or their partisans at Corinth, who formed a recognizable and influential segment of the church. He identifies them and their views in the following ways: "anyone" (10:7; 11:20–21), "some (people)" (10:2, 10, 12), "someone" (11:4), "those who" (11:12; 13:2), "such people" (10:11; 11:13), "Satan's servants" (11:15), "others" (10:13), "many" (11:18), "people" (13:7). On the other hand, "you" (plural, *hymeis; e.g.,*11:2; 13:11) always refers to the Corinthians in general, who were in danger of becoming infected with a foreign and destructive virus.

Throughout the section 10:1—11:15 there is a strong undercurrent of direct or indirect charges against these rivals. They are not submissive to Christ; they lack authority from the Lord; they have no God-assigned sphere of operation in Corinth but boast of their success there; they promulgate a different gospel; they are a financial burden on the Corinthians; and so far from being apostles of Christ and agents of righteousness, they are in reality Satan's deputies and deceitful operators.

5. See the chart in Harris, *Second Epistle to the Corinthians,* 46.

(A) The Exercise of Apostolic Authority (10:1–18)

(i) The Potency of Apostolic Authority (10:1–11)
(ii) Legitimate Spheres of Activity and Boasting (10:12–18)

10:1–11

Here the apostle is responding to an impression about him that had gained currency at Corinth, namely, that he had two radically different *personae*—"Paul the bold" and "Paul the timid." Safely distant from Corinth, he was a man of bold authoritarianism as he wrote his letters (such as "the previous letter," 1 Corinthians, and the "severe letter"), but face-to-face he was a pathetically weak creature (10:1, 9–10). He corrects this caricature and serves notice on the Corinthians by assuring them that he is fully prepared, if necessary, to display confident boldness when he next visits (10:2, 11). In a series of metaphors drawn from military warfare (10:3–5), the justice system (10:6), and architecture (10:8), he affirms both his authority to act boldly and the overwhelming potency of such action.

10:12–18

Having reassured his converts of the reality and potency of his apostolic authority in general (10:1–11), Paul addresses the claims of the nameless persons, the "false apostles," the intruders from Judea, who had invaded his legitimate jurisdiction or sphere of activity in Corinth (10:13–15) and were commending themselves and boasting beyond proper limits (10:12, 16, 18) on the basis of work that he had done in Corinth (10:15–16). God had allotted to Paul a special assignment at Corinth and had confirmed this appointment by prospering his pioneer preaching in the city (10:13–14). Any boasting should be restricted to what the Lord has achieved (10:17).

The awkward syntax of parts of this paragraph (10:13, 15–16), along with the many repeated words or phrases and the frequent use of the negative "no/not," are testimony to Paul's emotional intensity as he vigorously defends the assigned territory (cf. Gal 2:1–10) that he regarded as "home soil."

(B) Boasting "as a Fool" (11:1—12:13)

    (i) A Plea for Tolerance (11:1–6)

    (ii) Financial Dependence and Independence (11:7–12)

    (iii) False Apostles (11:13–15)

    (iv) Justification for Foolish Boasting (11:16–21a)

    (v) Paul's Heritage and Trials (11:21b–29)

    (vi) Escape from Damascus (11:30–33)

    (vii) A Vision and its Aftermath (12:1–10)

    (viii) Proof of Apostleship (12:11–13)

11:1–6

Faced by the foolish boasting of his opponents (10:12–16) that seems to have swayed the gullible Corinthians (cf. 11:4) to champion their cause, Paul confronted a dilemma. If he himself refrained from boasting he would risk losing the Corinthians to a false gospel (11:4); if he adopted his rivals' techniques and indulged in a temporary foray into foolish boasting, he risked being misunderstood by the Corinthians and playing into the hands of his adversaries. Sensing that the latter option was the lesser of two evils, he chose the way of "a little bit of foolishness" (11:1), "a little boasting" (11:16), and pleads for his converts' tolerance (11:1). Much was at stake at this stage of Paul's relationship with the church. They might lose their spiritual virginity (11:2) and their sincere and pure devotion to Christ (11:3).

The "super apostles" to whom Paul compared himself favorably (11:5; cf. 12:11) should probably not be identified as the Corinthian view of Paul's rivals, the false apostles (11:13), but rather as his own ironical description of the exalted view of the Twelve in Jerusalem held by those false apostles.[6] Irony is elsewhere in evidence in chapters 11 and 12—see 11:4, 7, 19, 21; 12:11, 13.

11:7–12

In 1 Cor 9:3–18 Paul had established two basic principles about his finances: his right as an apostle to receive support from those who benefited from the spiritual seed he had sown; his right to forego that support if there were practical or theological reasons for doing so. Here in 2 Cor 11:7–12 he focuses on his motivation for financial independence of the Corinthians, which was to preach the gospel to them "free of charge" (11:7) and to avoid being a financial burden on them (11: 9). His rivals, on the other hand, were evidently among the "many" who were making a petty trade out of preaching (2:17) and were "devouring" the Corinthians (11:20). They wanted to goad Paul into altering his policy and accepting support so that the embarrassing difference between them could be eradicated. Paul, however, resolved not to surrender this advantage over his rivals (11:10, 12).

11:13–15

Paul now strips off the disguise of these Judaizing intruders from Judea and reveals their true identity—they in fact belong to Satan (11:15), not Christ (as they claimed, 10:7); they are part of Satan's nefarious task force (11:13), not agents of righteousness (11:15); they are false apostles, not apostles of Christ (11:13).

6. See Harris, *Second Epistle to the Corinthians*, 67–87, 746–47.

11:16–21a

Paul's embarrassed displeasure at having to play his opponents' "game" of boasting is shown by this third effort actually to begin boasting (10:8; 11:1, 16) and by his repeated apologetic explanations. He was wearing a fool's mask not at the Lord's direction (11:17) but because of the Corinthians' immaturity in being dazzled by the barefaced bragging (11:18) of the intruders about their pedigree and accomplishments. In paradoxical irony he confesses to being too weak to imitate his rivals' domination, exploitation, entrapment, haughtiness and insult in dealing with the Corinthians (11:20–21a).

11:21b–29

After giving two reminders of his folly (11:21b, 23), Paul proceeds to point out his equality with his rivals in bold boasting (11:21b) and in nationality and heritage (11:22); the expression "I too" or "so am I" (*kagō*) occurs four times in vv. 21b–22. Then he highlights his vast superiority in service and suffering (11:23–29); "I more so" (*hyper egō*) is the key expression in 11:23a. After the comparisons of 11:23b, he mentions the specific hardships he endured (11:24–25), the dangers he confronted (11:26), and the privations experienced (11:27). While none of the afflictions listed in 11:23–27 was a continuous experience, his anxious concern for all the churches (11:29) and his empathetic support for needy fellow believers (11:29) were daily pressures.

11:30–33

Proud boasting in a worldly fashion (11:18, 21b) is now over, but Paul's reluctant boasting continues, now with a focus on evidences of his weakness (11:30). After a prefaced oath as to his truthfulness (11:31), he cites the first of two prime instances of that weakness—a humiliating escape from Damascus in a basket through a window in the city wall (11:32–33).

12:1–10

The second dramatic evidence of Paul's weakness was his permanent receipt of a debilitating "thorn in the flesh." What triggered this receipt was an exhilarating ascent into the presence of God that occurred fourteen years previously (12:2), that is, about AD 43 by inclusive reckoning, during the ten so-called "silent years" (AD 35–45) that Paul spent in Syria and Cilicia (Gal 1:21) and to which Acts does not refer. He objectifies his experience by referring to himself as "a man in Christ" (12:2–4) because he is embarrassed at needing to boast (12:1) and in order to avoid suggesting that he was in any sense a special kind of Christian or that the vision added anything to his status as an apostle (12:6). The giving of the thorn, like the vision itself, was at God's initiative and for a spiritual purpose (12:3–4, 7). His thrice-repeated prayer to the Lord Jesus for the thorn's removal was answered by a promise of divine grace and Christ's power in the midst of his weaknesses (12:8–9).

12:11–13

These three verses form the conclusion to the "Fool's Speech" (11:1–12:13). Once again (cf. 11:5) he asserts his equality with the "superlative apostles" in Jerusalem (12:11), an equality shown by his patiently exhibiting at Corinth the marks of true apostleship by means of signs, wonders, and miracles (12:12). He reminds them also that he remained financially independent of them at that time—an "injury" for which he playfully asks forgiveness (12:13).

(C) The Planned Third Visit (12:14—13:10)

> (i) A Promise Not to Be Burdensome (12:14–18)
>
> (ii) Fears about the Corinthians' State (12:19–21)
>
> (iii) Warning of Impending Discipline (13:1–4)
>
> (iv) A Plea for Self-Examination (13:5–10)

The underlying purpose of the whole letter is to prepare the Corinthians for his forthcoming visit so that it might prove mutually beneficial and enjoyable, not painful.

12:14–18

As Paul announces his third visit (12:14), he makes two promises to the believers at Corinth: He will not alter his practice of not being a financial encumbrance on them (12:14); and he will very gladly spend his resources and all his energies for their spiritual benefit (12:15). Regarding his past conduct, he responds to the accusation that he had operated as an unscrupulous trickster through his agents in order to defraud them financially (12:16–18).

12:19–21

Paul assures the Corinthians that his overriding aim in writing was not self-defense but their edification (12:19). And their upbuilding was an urgent need, for he had a threefold fear about what might happen on his arrival—that there might be mutual disappointment and embarrassment (12:20a); that he might find evidence of factiousness and disharmony (12:20b); and that he might be humiliated before his converts and find many still unrepentant about their immoral behavior (12:21).

13:1–4

This section states what Paul surmised the Corinthians would not want him to be on his next visit—someone who administers punishment. But he sensed that the mere expression of his personal forebodings (12:20–21) would not be sufficient to shake the Corinthians from their lethargy about their sins. So he repeats a warning that he had given as he departed from Corinth after his second visit: "On my return I will not spare you" (13:2). This punitive action would give the Corinthians the proof they were demanding that he was Christ's spokesman and agent (13:3a). He then develops a comparison between the two states of Christ (weakness and power) and his own dual approach in dealing with the Corinthians (13:3b–4).

13:5–10

Within this paragraph Paul's emotions seem to oscillate between hope and fear regarding his converts at Corinth. He hopes that they will discover him to be "not unapproved" (13:6) and that on his forthcoming visit he can be "weak" (13:9a) by not having to deal with them severely, and he prays for their restoration to spiritual wholeness (13:9b). Yet he fears that after all he may have to act "with unrelenting severity" against any dissidents (13:10).

(D) Conclusion (13:11–13)

13:11–13

Here Paul includes all four of the customary elements found in his letter endings: exhortation (v. 11a), a peace benediction (v. 11b), greetings (v. 12; EVV vv. 12–13), and a grace benediction (v. 13; EVV v. 14). The final verse contains the most elevated trinitarian affirmation in the New Testament, with the order of persons reflecting the believer's experience—Jesus Christ, God the Father, the Holy Spirit.

Part Three:

The First Epistle of Clement of Rome to the Corinthians

I. *Introduction*

The First Epistle of Clement of Rome is so-called because there is a Second Epistle of Clement also included among the Apostolic Fathers, although this 2 Clement dates from a later time, is not a letter (but a sermon), and is not by Clement (but by some unknown presbyter).The letter we know as 1 Clement was highly regarded in the ancient church, witness the fact that it was included immediately after the book of Revelation in the fifth-century Greek manuscript Codex Alexandrinus that contains the entire Old and New Testaments. First Clement is probably the earliest extant Christian document outside the New Testament. Quotations and allusions in this letter indicate that at least two New Testament books (Romans and 1 Corinthians) were known to the author.[1]

II. *Authorship*

Ancient tradition (see Eusebius, *Church History* 4.23.11) and most manuscripts attribute the letter to Clement, apparently one of the group of overseers or presbyters who presided over the church at

---

1. Donald A. Hagner, *The Use of the Old and New Testaments in Clement of Rome* (Leiden: Brill, 1973), 237.

Rome. "The words *episcopos* ("overseer") and *presbyteros* ("elder") . . . are synonymes (*sic*) in Clement, as they are in the Apostolic writers."[2] Although this church leader is not the Clement mentioned in Philippians 4:3, he may have been the church's secretary responsible for correspondence, as referred to in the *Shepherd of Hermas* 8 (= *Visions* 2.4.3) (date uncertain). Certainly, from the point of view of Greek style, the letter appears to stem from the pen of a single author.

III. *Date*

In her book, *A Church in Crisis: Ecclesiology and Paraenesis in Clement of Rome*, Barbara E. Bowe suggests[3] that the outer limits for the dating of the letter are about AD 80 (the *terminus a quo*) and AD 140 (the *terminus ad quem*). But the majority of scholars opt more specifically for a date of AD 95–96, based on the reference in 1:1 to "the sudden and repeated calamities and reverses that have happened to us," which is taken to be an allusion to the persecution of the church in Rome during the final years of the Emperor Domitian's reign (AD 81–96) or the early period of Nerva's principate (AD 96–98). These "sudden and repeated" misfortunes apparently were sufficiently severe to prompt a delay in the Roman response to the serious crisis at Corinth (1:1). Intermittent acts of persecution could appropriately be termed both "repeated" and "sudden."

Other data relevant to dating are: (1) references to the deaths of Peter and Paul (that occurred in the mid–60s) (5:3–7). (2) Mention is made in 42:2–5 of the appointment of "overseers and deacons" by the apostles of Christ. Then 44:1–3 alludes to a succession of "other approved men" who served as presbyters, which implies

2. J. B. Lightfoot, *The Apostolic Fathers. Part I. S. Clement of Rome* (Grand Rapids: Baker, 1981), 129.

3. Barbara E. Bowe, *A Church in Crisis: Ecclesiology and Paraenesis in Clement of Rome* (Minneapolis: Fortress, 1988), 2–3.

a considerable passage of time. (3) The men sent by the Roman church as messengers to report back on the response to the letter at Corinth (65:1) are described as having lived blameless lives "from youth to old age" (63:3). (4) The Corinthian church is described as being "ancient" (47:6).

IV. Text

The primary sources for the Greek text of 1 Clement are five in number.

1. Codex Alexandrinus (fifth century) which lacks 57:7—63:4
2. Codex Hierosolymitanus (AD 1056), the only complete text
3. A Latin translation (probably from the second or third century)
4. A Syriac translation
5. An incompletely preserved Coptic translation

A splendid modern translation of the text, based on J. B. Lightfoot's rendering,[4] may be found in Holmes.[5] All the citations from the letter in what follows are my own translation.

V. *Purpose and Content* (1 Clem 54:2)

In its essence the letter is an urgent appeal by the church at Rome to the church in Corinth to revive their good reputation by rejecting factionalism and pursuing communal peace and harmony, and by reinstating their honorable elders who had been deposed by an aggressive group of younger believers. Of these two emphases in the letter, the former is regarded as the more important.[6]

---

4. Lightfoot, *Apostolic Fathers*, 271–305.

5. Michael W. Holmes, *The Apostolic Fathers. Greek Texts and English Translations* (Grand Rapids: Baker, 2007), 45–131 (or the almost identical earlier translation published in 1989, 28–64).

6. Similarly Bowe, *Church in Crisis*, 22–23, 155.

If there is one sentence in the letter that aptly sums up its purpose and content, it is found in 54:2.

"Let the flock of Christ live peaceably with its duly appointed presbyters."

It may be noted that the crucial verb in this verse (*eirēneuō*) is precisely parallel to Rom 12:18 ("live peaceably with everyone"), having the same present tense and being followed by the same preposition (*meta*, "with"). In these two verses this verb means "keep the peace" (so BDF 287c), "be at peace" (so Lightfoot 299 on 1 Clem 54:2) or "live peaceably" (so KJV and NRSV on Rom 12:18). In 1 Clem 63:4 the aorist tense of the verb is found: "Our whole concern has been, and still is, that you should speedily attain peace."

Using this thematic statement we may make several observations about the letter's purpose and content that are validated by numerous references elsewhere.

A. *The letter reads as a potent exhortation*, not a mandatory directive: "Let the flock of Christ live peaceably." The Roman leadership recognized that they had no special authority over their fellow believers in Corinth; they could only appeal to them in brotherly love.

Clearly the believers in Rome were intently anxious for the recovery of the splendid reputation of the Corinthians. "Your name, once so revered and extolled and admirable in the sight of everyone, has been greatly reviled" (1:1). It was this warm commendation of the Corinthians' reputation (1:1—2:8; 47:5) that prompted the equally fervent exhortation for them to eradicate "the disgusting and unholy schism, so alien and strange to those chosen by God" (1:1). Naturally, this exhortation was accompanied by the Romans' fervent prayer for the end of the sedition and the return of peace and concord (56:1; 60:4; 65:1), and for the preservation of those adversely affected by the schism (59:4, "Save those of us who are in distress;" cf. 46:9).

Yet alongside the repeated exhortations there were sometimes other approaches.

(i) V*igorous commands*: "Root out this (stupidity) quickly" (48:1). "You will give us joy and happiness if you obey what we have written through the Holy Spirit and root out the lawless anger of your jealousy, action that will accord with the appeal for peace and harmony that we have made in this letter" (63:2).

(ii) *Appeals to Christian obligation.* "The greater a person seems to be . . . the more they ought to seek the advantage of all, and not their own" (48:6).

(iii) *Direct reproof.* "Let us accept correction. Receiving it should displease no one, dear friends. Indeed, the reproof we give one another is appropriate and very useful, for it unites us with the will of God" (56:2).

But whatever technique was employed to encourage change, it was applied with a certain gentleness. "Accept our advice, and you will have no reason for regret" (58:2). "Let us hurry to return to the goal of peace" (19:2). "Let us be kind to them (the instigators of the schism), for this accords with the compassion and sweetness of the One who made us" (14:3).

B. *The letter was addressed to the whole Corinthian church,* "the flock of Christ," not merely the instigators of the revolt against leadership. On occasion the exhortation is addressed directly to the offenders but generally the addressees are all the believers in Corinth.

Evidence of this corporate address is found not only in the frequent first person plural exhortations (e.g., "Let us abandon empty and pointless thoughts and let us follow the glorious and holy rule of our tradition," 7:2) but also in the repeated use of inclusive terms indicating brotherhood and affection: the vocative plural *adelphoi* ("brothers [and sisters]") occurs some fourteen times, while the parallel *agapētoi* ("dear friends") is used some seventeen times. In fact, both expressions are found in the long first sentence (1:1) that follows the brief salutation.

Guilt for the factiousness in the church is laid at the door of the whole congregation. "We see that you (plural) have removed certain people (the appointed presbyters), in spite of their good conduct, from the ministry that had been exercised by them honorably and blamelessly" (44:6). In a similar way we find references to "your schism" (46:9) and "your stupidity" (47:7). On occasion the writers go so far as to identify themselves with the erring church. "Let us ask to be forgiven for whatever sins we have committed and whatever actions we have carried out through any of the tricks of the adversary" (51:1; similarly 21:1).

In 57:1–2 there is a direct confrontation of the troublemakers. "You who laid the foundation of the sedition, must submit to the presbyters and accept the discipline that leads to repentance by bending the knees of your heart. Learn how to submit yourselves, setting aside the arrogant and proud stubbornness of your tongue." And although 56:6 is a quotation of Job 5:17, it clearly has in mind the offending of the agitators. "Blessed is the person whom the Lord reproves; do not reject the warning of the Almighty."

C. *The root cause of the disunity at Corinth* was the successful effort of several young men to dislodge the elders from their position.

It is unclear how many people were directly involved in instigating the revolt, since references to them are vague; perhaps the writers themselves were uncertain.

"a few headstrong and stubborn persons" (1:1)

"people were stirred up: those without honor against the honored, those without repute against the highly reputed, the foolish against the wise, the young men against the elders" (3:3, citing Isa 3:5)

"those imagined leaders who have acted in arrogance, anarchy, and abominable jealousy" (14:1)

"people who launch out into strife and sedition so as to alienate us from what is proper" (14:2)

"those who hypocritically desire peace" (15:1)

"Let the treacherous lips that speak evil against the righteous become speechless" (15:5, citing Ps 30:19, LXX)

"those who exalt themselves over his (Christ's) flock" (16:1)

"foolish and senseless people who exalt themselves and boast arrogantly in their words" (21:5)

"those who praise themselves" (30:6)

"Boldness and arrogance and audacity mark those who are cursed by God" (30:8)

"those who have turned you aside and sullied the good reputation arising from your renowned brotherly love" (47:5)

"one or two persons" (47:6)

"those who became leaders of rebellion and division" (51:1)

"certain people" (59:1)

What is clear from these characterizations is that the presbyters or elders who were displaced by nameless young people were regarded (at least by the leaders at Rome) as righteous and wise men of honor and high repute, while their usurpers were arrogant upstarts who were motivated by foolish jealousy and were spreading malicious gossip about the elders in what amounted to "rebellion" (46:9; 47:6). Apparently there were within the church some who sympathized with the agitators. "Those who do these things (lawlessness, strife, gossip etc., 35:5) are loathed by God; and not only those who do these things but also those who approve of them" (35:6).

Horrell defends the view[7] that the deposed elders belonged to the more socially prominent sections of the community as heads of households, while the agitators came from a lower social status.

7. David G. Horrell, *The Social Ethos of the Corinthian Correspondence: Interests and Ideology from 1 Corinthians to 1 Clement* (Edinburgh: T. & T. Clark, 1996), 250, 279.

It is sometimes questioned (as by Bowe[8]) whether the leaders of the revolt were in fact young people. 1 Clem 3:3 reads "people were stirred up: those lacking honor against the honored, those without repute against the highly reputed, the foolish against the wise, the young against the elder." In these four parallel phrases the first and the fourth are based on Isa 3:5b in the LXX: "a child/ young person (*to paidion*) will be angry at his elder, the person lacking honor will be angry at the honored." Given this first phrase in Isa 3:5b, it seems highly probable that the traditional view is correct—the agitators were younger members of the Corinthian congregation.

D. *A clarion call for harmony to replace schism at Corinth*, for a return to an earlier time when "every sedition and every schism was disgusting in your eyes" (2:6).

> "Why is there strife and bursts of anger and divisions and schisms among you?" (46:5)

> "Let us join with those who reverently practice peace" (15:1). "Seek peace and pursue it" (22:5)

> "Love does not create schism, love produces no revolts, love does everything in harmony" (49:5)

> "Even the most insignificant of living things come together in concord and peace" (20:10)

> ". . . the appeal for peace and harmony that we have made in this letter" (63:2)

Any such disharmony was totally incompatible with the oneness of the Body of Christ. "Why do we tear and rip apart the members of Christ and rise in rebellion against our own body, and reach such a height of folly that we actually forget that we are members of one another?" (46:7; cf. 37:5).

To achieve this grand reversal to previous times of mutual submission (2:1), or for this restoration to "honorable and pure conduct" (48:1) to take place, the leaders of the revolt "must submit to the presbyters and accept discipline that will lead to repentance"

8. Bowe, *Church in Crisis*, 18–19.

(57:1; cf. 7:5—8:5). "Learn how to be submissive, laying aside the arrogant and proud stubbornness of your speech" (57:2). "It is right for us . . . to side with those who are the leaders of our souls" (63:1). "Let us honor our elders" (21:6). Presumably this alignment with the elders involved reinstating them to their rightful status and office.

Failure to repent and accept the divine reproof, "the correction of the Almighty" (56:6), would lead to serious consequences.

> "Since all things are seen and heard (by God, 27:6), let us fear him and abandon the detestable desires that lead to evil works, so that we may be sheltered by his mercy from the coming judgments" (28:1).

> "Accept our advice and you will have no occasion for regret (58:2) . . . but if certain people were to disobey what has been said by him (God) through us, let them understand that they will entangle themselves in serious sin and grave danger" (59:1).

Scattered throughout the letter are appeals to scriptural examples, usually from the OT since most of the NT documents were unavailable to the authors. These examples are cited to support the central exhortations.[9] Instances of these relevant appeals include the following passages.

1. Repentance

"Let us review all the previous generations and learn that in generation after generation the Master has provided a chance for repentance to those who desired to turn to him. Noah preached repentance, and those who obeyed were saved. Jonah preached destruction to the people of Nineveh, but those who repented of their sins gained God's pardon through prayer and received salvation although they had been alienated from God" (7:5-7). "The Master of the universe himself spoke about repentance, using an oath: 'For as I live, says the Lord, I do not desire the death of the sinner, but rather his repentance'" (8:2).

---

9. An authoritative treatment of this matter may be found in Hagner, *Clement of Rome.*

2. Humility

"Let us be imitators also of those who went about in goatskins and sheepskins, preaching the coming of Christ. We mean Elijah and Elisha, and in a similar way Ezekiel, the prophets, and along with them those who were well renowned. Abraham was extremely well renowned and was called the 'friend of God;' yet when he gazed intently at the glory of God, he said in humility, 'I am simply dust and ashes'" (17:1–2).

"The humility and submissiveness of so many people who were so well renowned have made not only us better but also the generations before us, as a result of their obedience" (19:1).

3. Obedience

"Let us fix our gaze on those who perfectly served his superlative glory. Let us consider Enoch, for example, who was found righteous because of his obedience and was taken up and did not experience death" (9:2–3). "Abraham, who was named 'the friend,' was found faithful in that he became obedient to the words of God. In obedience he ventured out from his country . . ." (10:1–2).

4. Jealousy

"You see, brothers, jealousy and envy brought about the murder of a brother (Abel). Because of (Esau's) jealousy our father Jacob ran away from the presence of his brother Esau. Jealousy caused Joseph to be persecuted almost to death and actually to be sold into slavery (4:7–9).

5. Judgment

"The Master . . . appoints to punishment and torment those who turn aside. His (Lot's) wife was appointed to be a sign of this, for after leaving (Sodom) with him she altered her outlook and no longer agreed (with Lot), and as a result she became a pillar of salt to this day, so that it might be known to everyone that those who are double-minded and those who doubt the power of God are destined for judgment and serve as a warning to all generations" (11:1–2).

Part Four:

Lessons for the Twenty-First-Century Church

In no sense should the following lessons be seen as a partial summary of the theological and practical teaching found in Paul's two Corinthian letters and in 1 Clement. Summaries of Paul's teaching and instruction, and that of the anonymous author of 1 Clement, were given earlier. Rather, these lessons are an effort to isolate features of Paul's practical ministry in Corinth and aspects of the history of the Corinthian church itself that may prove beneficial for twenty-first-century churches and their leaders to consider and then follow. That is, *the focus is on what actually happened and may prove exemplary, not on what ought to occur or should have happened.*

I. *Features of the Corinthian Church Worthy of Perpetual Imitation*

These features are clear from passages in all three documents.

The only place in 1 Corinthians where Paul explicitly praises the Corinthians is 11:2 where he commends them for adhering to Christian traditions—in this context perhaps Paul's teaching about the participation of women in prayer and prophecy during public worship. As for 2 Corinthians, in 3:3 Paul's converts at Corinth are said to demonstrate openly that they are a letter composed by Christ and transcribed by Paul himself. Then in 9:2 they are applauded for their eagerness and enthusiasm to help with Paul's relief project for Jerusalem. But the most detailed passage is Paul's report in 2 Cor 7:6–13 of the church's positive response to his "severe letter" as described by his representative Titus. They had consoled Titus (2 Cor 7:7a, 13) who was the bearer of this embarrassing letter (2 Cor 7:8–9) and had explained and clarified for them its contents and demands (see above, III. C.). They were ardently devoted to Paul (2 Cor 7:7b, 12b) as their spiritual father (cf. 1 Cor 4:15) who had reluctantly considered it necessary to reprove them (2 Cor 7: 8). They painfully recognized the error of their ways and their need for correction, and their "godly sorrow" produced genuine repentance and an eager longing to clear themselves of culpability (2 Cor 7:9–11).

The first two chapters of 1 Clement are given over to a recitation of exemplary aspects of the church's recent history—before addressing in the remaining sixty-three chapters the distressing behavior that was so unlike their good reputation. These exemplary aspects included steadfast faith, sober Christian piety, generous hospitality (1:2), commitment to the laws of God (1:3; 2:8), submission to leaders (1:3; 2:1), giving appropriate instruction to the young and to women (1:3), pleasure in giving, contentment with God's provision (2:1), an insatiable desire to do good (2:2, 7), vigorous effort on behalf of the brotherhood, and freedom from malice toward one another (2:4–5).

II. *Potential Schism as a Perennial Problem*

It was not only in the fifties of the first century AD but also in the nineties that *schism* occurred and produced relational problems within the Corinthian church (1 Cor 1:10–4:21; 2 Cor 12:20–13:2; 1 Clem 46:1—48:6; 51:1—53:5). In fact 1 Clement reminds its readers or hearers of this earlier history: "Even then you had split into factions" (47:3).

The mere fact that a particular congregation was founded and built up by a distinguished rabbinical scholar turned apostle of Christ, or another church is now renowned for its influential pastor or priest who enjoys a worldwide TV or writing ministry, is no guarantee that church will be unified and free of inter-personal problems. Any Christian church is composed of people who have all the frailties and propensities of human life, even though the Spirit of Christ is active in and among them. We should never imagine that a church's famous or outstanding past or its illustrious leader makes certain its problem-free future. Recognizing this should make us constantly aware of "danger ahead" and should generate prayer for unity and constant humility (see also IV. below).

III. *Recognizing the Cunning Tactics of the Devil*

Both Paul and the author(s) of 1 Clement recognized that believers were combatting "spiritual forces of evil in the heavenly realms" (Eph 6:12). Accordingly, the apostle speaks of avoiding being outwitted by Satan, "for we are not unaware of his stratagems" (2 Cor 2:11). In the case of "the one who had caused grief" (2 Cor 2:5), a majority of the Corinthians had imposed some unstated form of punishment that Paul now says is sufficient lest the man be overwhelmed by excessive sorrow (2 Cor 2:6–7). Failure to forgive and comfort this person would play into Satan's hands (2 Cor 2:7, 11). Elsewhere the apostle emphasizes the need to "put on the full armor that God supplies so that you may be able to stand firm against *the cunning tactics/deceitful craftiness of the devil*" (Eph 6:11). And 1 Clement refers to sins that have been committed "because of any of the tricks of the adversary" (1 Clem 51:1). In two of these references to the devil's schemes (viz. 2 Cor 2:11; 1 Clem 51:1), the context relates to actual or potential division within the church. Clearly, then, one of Satan's principal aims is to create schism in the local church; his purposes are diametrically opposed to those of Christ (2 Cor 6:15, "What harmony is there between Christ and Belial?"). One reason Satan's schemes are so cunning is that he specializes in masquerading as an angel of light (2 Cor 11:14).

How are believers or Christian communities to "extinguish all the flaming missiles of the evil one" (Eph 6:16, NASB) and avoid being "deceived by the serpent's cunning" (2 Cor 11:3)? By putting on the complete armament that God supplies (Eph 6:11–17), by maintaining "a sincere and pure devotion to Christ" (2 Cor 11:3), and by extending forgiveness and reinstatement to any repentant offender (2 Cor 2:5–11). In this latter regard, we must remember that even after forgiveness is offered and received, the offender may have to live with any inevitable consequences of their actions, so that ongoing counselling could be needed.

IV. *Dealing with Interpersonal Conflict*

In the two main literary stages of the Corinthian church (the 50s and the 90s), *conflict between members* was dealt with in a similar way, with Paul and the author(s) of First Clement operating at a distance and communicating by letter, reinforced by delegates (Timothy, 1 Cor 4:17; 16:10; Titus, 2 Cor 7: 6–7, 13–14; 12:17–18; Claudius Ephebus and Valerius Bito, 1 Clem 63:3; 65:1).

What Paul and First Clement had in common was the way they confronted interpersonal conflict and division—with an appeal to unchanging theological truths and Christian obligations.

- The oneness of the body of Christ, that made division incongruous (1 Cor 1:10, 13; 6:15, 17; 8:6; 10:17; 12:12–27; 1 Clem 46:6–7, "Do we not have one God and one Christ and one Spirit of grace who was poured out on us? And is there not one calling in Christ? Why do we pull apart and tear the members of Christ, and rise in rebellion against our own body, and reach such a height of insanity that we forget we are members of one another?").

- The primacy of love, especially as promoting harmony (1 Cor 13: 1–13; 16:14; 1 Clem 49:5, "Love knows nothing of schisms, love creates no sedition, love carries out everything in harmony"; 50:5, "the harmony of love").

- Repudiate divisions (1 Cor 3:3–4; 11:18–22; 1 Clem 48:1; 50:2; 54:1–2).

- Embrace humility (1 Cor 4:18–19; 2 Cor 10:1; 1 Clem 16:1; 17:1–2; 30:3, 7; 56:1) and purity (1 Cor 1:8; 2 Cor 7:1; 1 Clem 29:1; 30:1, 8).

- Repent of sin (2 Cor 7:10–11; 12:21; 1 Clem 7:5; 8:2, 5).

- Become submissive and obedient (1 Cor 16:15–16; 2 Cor 2:9; 10:6; 1 Clem 9:2–3; 10:1–2; 14:1; 63:1).

- Recognize God's discipline (1 Cor 11:30–32; 1 Clem 56:2–6, 16; 57:1).

Even when there is no distance between leader and subject(s) and so no delegates are needed, these appeals just mentioned are applicable. But additional techniques for dealing with division are available when face-to-face contact is possible. In some cases, leaders must "keep an eye on" (*skopein*) and simply "avoid" (*ekklinete*) or cut off all relations with "those who are causing division" by actively propagating false teaching and so deceiving immature believers (Rom 16:17–18). On the other hand, in Matt 18:15–20 Jesus sets out four general procedures that may be followed when dealing with strife within a congregation as well as the specific circumstance Jesus had in mind. (1) The individuals involved should seek mutual reconciliation (Matt 18:15). (2) If one party resists reconciliation, other persons should be brought in to serve as witnesses to the negotiations and as facilitators of reconciliation (Matt 18:16). (3) If the offending party remains unrepentant, the whole congregation may be informed and apply pressure on the offender to create reconciliation and harmony (Matt 18:7a). (4) If even this pressure is unsuccessful, the offending and unrepentant party should face social ostracism (Matt 18:17b) for the preservation and good of the whole community. Also, when inter-personal conflict is present, there could be a place for the formal appointment of skillful mediators (see above) who seek to resolve the issues involved and restore harmony within the church. A productive place to start is for all the parties involved to pray together and express their oneness in Christ.

Certainly, before any recourse is had to secular facilities, whether legal or social, every effort must be made to settle grievances using talent within the local church (cf. 1 Cor 6:1–6) such as elders or deacons or an "elder statesman" such as a retired businessman.

V. *Accommodating Vocal Young People*

It appears that in the mid-nineties of the first century the Corinthian church included in its congregation *a vocal group of younger people* (presumably men) who had initiated a revolt against the established and highly respected elders and had somehow succeeded in deposing them (1 Clem 3:3; 14:1–2; 21:5–6; 44:4, 6; 46:5, 9; 47:5–6). The details of the uprising, its motivation and its stages, are unknown.

Church leadership, whether pastors, deacons, elders, or priests, should establish regular contact with representatives of younger members of the congregation to address any concerns they may have about church life and future plans, as well as about wider non-church issues.

This regular contact could be achieved:

(i) by having the leader of the youth serve on the eldership *ex officio* or as an "elder in training," or at least be invited to attend eldership meetings as an observer or a non-voting participant; and

(ii) by having an advertised way by which needs or concerns among the young people can be registered with the leadership by anyone, whether anonymously or by name.

Also, where a church's constitution exists, there should be unambiguously stated the means by which an elder or deacon is appointed or may be removed from office, whether by those already holding the office or by collective church vote. Also, an agreed rotation of eldership ensures both innovation and continuity.

Other ways in which the distinctive needs of young people and young families could be met include the following:

- a second later Sunday service with more contemporary music, facilities for infants and younger children, but with the same sermon (although a regular united service for young and old would be needed to express the unity of the congregation)

- a midweek evening gathering to discuss issues that arise from the sermon

- a monthly evangelistic meeting in the evening that addresses local or national concerns from a Christian viewpoint

- weekly fitness classes or games competitions

VI. *Encouraging Submission to Leadership*

The only explicit call in the Corinthian letters for submission to certain people is found in 1 Cor 15:16: "I urge you, brothers and sisters . . . to submit to people such as these (the household of Stephanas) and to everyone who works and toils with them," although Eph 5:21 sums up Paul's general stance: "Submit to one another out of reverence for Christ." In 1 Clement, on the other hand, the plea to the agitators to submit to their God-appointed elders is at the heart of the letter. "You who laid the foundation of the uprising must submit to your elders and accept discipline that will lead to repentance, bending the knees of your heart. Learn how to be submissive" (1 Clem 57:1–2).

This prompts the suggestion that on (at least) an annual basis a sermon should be delivered about the Christian's obligation to submit to the God-appointed leadership of the church. Ideally, this sermon would be preached by a capable and respected layperson within the church; or perhaps by a highly regarded visitor such as a regional or denominational leader. For example, such a sermon could be based on Heb 12:1–3; 13:1–17.

"'Follow the Leader': Child's Play or Christian Calling?"

1. Follow the Leader and run the race (12:2)

2. Remember your past leaders and imitate their faith (13:7)

3. Obey your present leaders and submit to their authority (13:17)

In developing this easily misunderstood theme of submission, one could first of all discuss the example of Christ who was and is subordinate to his Father (1 Cor 11:3; 15:28) while retaining his essential equality and parity of status with the Father.

At the conclusion of such a sermon, there could be corporate prayer in which congregational leaders publicly submit themselves to the Lord of the Church, before the congregation as a whole submit themselves to their leaders who are recognized as Christ's appointees so that submission to them is regarded as submission to Christ.

VII. *Church Interdependence*

For some five years (AD 52–57) Paul seems to have be preoccupied with organizing an offering among his Gentile churches for "the poor among God's people in Jerusalem" (Rom 15:26). Given his awkward relationship with the believers in Jerusalem owing to his earlier ruthless persecution of the infant church there (Acts 9:1–2; 22:4–5; Gal 1:13), it is not surprising that he had some unease about the success of this enterprise: "Pray that . . . my relief mission for Jerusalem may be favorably received by the Lord's people there" (Rom 15:31). Although there is no specific mention in Acts of the reaction in Jerusalem to the receipt of the collection, Acts 21:17 suggests that the gifts were gratefully received: "When we arrived at Jerusalem, the brothers and sisters welcomed us warmly" (see also under 2 Cor 9:12–15).

Did the Corinthian church play its part in contributing to this *relief mission*? From several references in 2 Corinthians (viz. 8:6, 10–11; 9:5), it is clear they had made an auspicious start, so that

Paul's concern was that they should "bring to completion this act of grace" (2 Cor 8:6). Evidently, in the five or so months between the writing of 2 Corinthians (Fall AD 56) and Romans (early AD 57) they had responded to their spiritual father's appeals, for in Rom 15:26–27 he writes, "Macedonia and Achaia (= Corinth) have been pleased to make a contribution for the poor among God's people in Jerusalem. Yes, they were pleased to do this. . ."

What, then, is the wider significance of this innovative foray into international relief aid? Here, remarkably, we see widely scattered Gentile Christian communities within the Roman empire (viz. from Macedonia, Galatia, Asia [Acts 20:4], and Achaia) creating a relief package for some needy Jewish brothers and sisters in Christ whom they had never met.

In the twenty-first century, all churches, especially those in the affluent West, should establish and develop *a relationship with needy and perhaps smaller churches*, crossing over cultural or national boundaries. That needy church could be a struggling inner-city congregation or a church abroad that faces constant persecution. Representatives of the "mother church" could regularly visit the adopted "daughter church" to deliver an accumulated gift in person, provide teaching, and stimulate local initiatives in self-employment and evangelism, and then report back to the sending congregation. In this regard, note the roles of Epaphroditus (Phil 4:18), the unnamed brother of 2 Cor 8:18–19, the church representatives mentioned in Acts 20:4, and the two delegates of 1 Clem 65:1.

This is not to question the ideal that every church should be self-supporting, self-governing and self-propagating, but sensitive help in achieving this ideal is never out of place. Any relationship between churches should ideally be mutual. Mothers benefit from the advice, wisdom and challenge of daughters! Now that the numerical center of gravity in the Christian world has shifted to Africa and Latin America, hopefully this reciprocity will develop more and more rapidly. In many modern secular societies there is a splendid precedent for such a reciprocal relationship when one town or city is partnered with a similar overseas equivalent, prompting mutual visits and support, such as regular student exchanges.

VIII. *Instruction about Christian Stewardship*

Nowhere in Scripture is there a more comprehensive treatment of Christian stewardship than in chapters 8 and 9 of 2 Corinthians. See our earlier discussion of these passages. Here we shall examine Paul's detailed instructions on the matter found in 1 Cor 16:2, realizing that the believers at Corinth probably followed these specific directions as they responded to his persistent appeal. As Paul prepares for this forthcoming visit (1 Cor 4:18–19; 16:5–6), he repeats directions already given to his Galatian churches (cf. Acts 18:23) so that there would be no need for special collections to be made after his arrival (1 Cor 16:1, 2b).

> "On the first day of every week, each one of you should set aside at home and store up a sum of money in proportion to how they are prospering" (1 Cor 16:2)

From these directions we can deduce five characteristics of Christian giving according to Paul. The following five points reflect material that appeared in my book, *Navigating Tough Texts*[1] and is used with permission.

(1). *Regular.* "On the first day of every week" (cf. John 20:1, 19; Acts 20:7) = "every Sunday," perhaps in preparation for meeting on "the Lord's Day" (Rev 1:10). "Should set aside" (*titheto*) is a present imperative implying "let this be your habit."

(2). *Individual and private.* Although any formal collecting of the gifts might be done in public, the "setting aside" was the responsibility of each individual person, acting "at home" (*par' heautō*) and so avoiding any competitiveness.

(3). *Voluntary.* Paul is not issuing a formal command, for giving cannot be mandated. As he says later regarding this

---

1. Murray J. Harris, *Navigating Tough Texts* (Bellingham, WA: Lexham, 2020) 135–36.

collection, "I am not commanding you" (2 Cor 8:8) and "I am simply giving you my advice" (2 Cor 8:10).

(4). *Financial.* The use of the technical term *logeia* ("collection") in 1 Cor 16:1 refers to money, so that the "storing up" or "saving" of v. 2 relates to money, not goods.

(5). *Proportional.* The phrase "in proportion to how they are prospering" does not refer to profit or income—there were slaves in the Corinthian church—nor to "whatever they can afford" or "as much as they can spare," but refers to general financial prospering week by week. The "proportion" is not some specific percentage but conformity to whatever degree of prosperity individuals have enjoyed. Again, in the same context Paul says "as resources permit" (2 Cor 8:11) or "in proportion to what one has" (2 Cor 8:12).

In his extensive discussion of this "collection for the poor" (some 43 verses: 1 Cor 16:1-4; 2 Cor 8-9), why does Paul not refer to tithing in support of his appeals to the Corinthians to bring their "charitable work" (*charis,* 2 Cor 8:19) to a successful conclusion? How would he regard the widespread encouragement and practice of tithing in the Christian world?

Over the centuries many believers and churches have been spiritually invigorated when individuals began to honor God by tithing. Also, tithers tend to be better stewards of the nine tenths than non-tithers are of the ten tenths. Undoubtedly, we may regard the practice of tithing as a splendid starting point in the adventure of giving to God.

However, the uniform NT emphasis falls on the need to give voluntarily, generously and proportionately (see, for example, Luke 21:4; Acts 11:28-30; 2 Cor 8:2-4, 11-13; 9:5-7; Eph 4:28; 1 Tim 6:18; Heb 13:16) in response to God's limitless giving (2 Cor 8:8-9; 9:15; 1 John 3:17). An appeal to Jewish tradition to support tithing overlooks the fact that there was a "triple tithe" in OT times: (1) a tithe to the Levites (Num 18:21-32); (2) a produce tithe (Lev 27:30-33; Deut 12:17-18; 14:22-26); (3) a charity tithe, paid every three years (Deut 14:28-29). Even if these tithes overlapped or varied in different times and places, it is unlikely the OT tithe amounted to merely 10 percent; it may have been over 20 percent and was a tax, not a freewill offering. An appeal to Mal 3:7–10 often ignores the ominous curse of v. 9 for withholding tithes. The three NT passages (Matt 23:23 [= Luke 11:42]; Luke 18:12; Heb 7:4–6, 8–9) that explicitly refer to tithing presuppose the OT era and economy, not NT times. Only the portions of OT law explicitly reaffirmed in the NT are part of "the law of Christ" (Gal 6:2), but tithing is nowhere re-imposed in the NT.

From an economic point of view, to impose tithing (regarded as the giving of 10 percent of all one's income) as a Christian *duty*, is to perpetuate a "rich—poor" inequality, for (at least in the West) tithing favors the rich and penalizes the poor. Christian stewardship relates to 100 percent of one's life and possessions, not merely a percentage. In practice, fastidious tithing can easily lead us to imagine that the nine tenths is ours to use as we want, not God's. But with this said, it is unquestionably true that the practice of tithing has brought untold spiritual benefit to many individuals and churches, so that it can be confidently proposed as an admirable way of honouring God.

The physical presentation of our offering is itself part of our worship. In the twenty-first century, when gifts are often given using modern technology, would it not be appropriate to place a "gold coin" in the offering bag as a tangible and visual symbol of our devotion to God? It is distressing to see such receptacles passed along rows only to be met by the polite shaking of heads. Even children could be encouraged to give a portion of their weekly or monthly allowance in this visible way.

All of this prompts the proposal that on an annual basis teaching should be given on Christian stewardship, again ideally by a suitably qualified lay person, lest the leadership be appearing to feather their own nest! Here is a sample comprehensive sermon outline that could prove helpful to the person entrusted with the task of addressing the church on this topic. This outline, used with permission, reproduces my article, "Christian Stewardship," that appeared in *Interest,* a magazine that ceased to be published in 1996.[2]

CHRISTIAN STEWARDSHIP

1. Its Nature

(i) The receiving and sharing of God's gifts (1 Chr 29:14, 16; Matt 10:8; 1 Tim 6:6–7; 1 Pet 4:10), especially the Good News (1 Cor 4:1; 9:16–18; Eph 3:1–9; Col :25–26), for the glory of God and the benefit of others (1 Cor 12:7; 2 Cor 8:19; 9:13).

(ii) An act of worship (Acts 10:4, 31; Rom 12:1; Phil 4:18; Heb 13:16) and of Christian fellowship (2 Cor 8:4; 9:13) and service (2 Cor 9:12–13).

(iii) An expression of God's grace (2 Cor 8:1–2, 6–7; 9:14) and of our dedication to Christ (2 Cor 8:4–5).

2. Its Scope

(i) Every Christian is a steward—whether rich (1 Tim 6:8–10, 17–19; 1 John 3:17) or poor (2 Cor 8:1–2), male or female (Acts 9:36, 39; Rom 12:13; 1 Tim 5:10; Tit 1:8).

(ii) All of life is a trust from God, not simply our possessions (1 Cor 4:7).

3. Its Motivation

(i) Attitude is all-important, for this determines whether or not a gift we give is acceptable to God (Acts 5:1–11; 1 Cor 13:3; Heb 11:4; cf. Gen 4:1–7).

(ii) The example of Christ (2 Cor 5:14; 8:9; 9:15) and our gratitude to him (John 15:12; 1 John 4:19).

---

2. Murray J. Harris, "Christian Stewardship" (*Interest* [February 1979], 4–5).

(iii) Repayment of a spiritual debt in material terms (Rom 15:26–27; 1 Cor 9:3–14; Gal 6:6; 1 Tim 5:17–18).

(iv) Future accountability (Rom 14:10–12; 1 Cor 4:2; 2 Cor 5:10; cf. Luke 16:1–2).

(v) The need for equality in the provision of the necessities of life (Deut 15:7–8; 2 Cor 8:13–15; cf. Matt 25:31–46).

4. Its Exercise

(i)   Voluntary, not enforced (Exod 25:1–2; 1 Cor 16:2; 2 Cor 8:3; 9:5, 7).

(ii)   Generous, not parsimonious (2 Chr 24:8–11; 2 Cor 8:2; 9:6, 13; 1 Tim 6:18).

(iii) Enthusiastic, not grudging (2 Cor 8:4, 11–12; 9:7).

(iv)   Deliberate, not haphazard (Act 11:29; 2 Cor 9:7).

(v)   Regular, not spasmodic (1 Cor 16:2).

(vi)   Sensible, not reckless (Exod 36:1–7; Deut 16:17; Acts 4:34–35; 5:4; 11:29; 1 Cor 16:2; 2 Cor 8:11–12).

(vii) Creative, not unimaginative (Luke 16:1–9).

(viii) Unobtrusive, not ostentatious (Matt 6:1–4; but see Acts 4:35; 5:2; 2 Cor 8:24).

(ix)   In God's power (Phil 4:10–13; 1 Pet 4:11).

5. Its Results

(i) The praise of God (2 Cor 9:11–13).

(ii) The needs of others are met (2 Cor 8:14; 9:12) and an example is afforded them (2 Cor 8:1–5; 9:2).

(iii) The multiplication of resources for further giving (2 Cor 9:8–10; Phil 4:19).

(iv) Answered prayer (Prov 21:13; Isa 58:1–12; 1 John 3:17–22).

(v) Personal enrichment and reward (Matt 6:4; Acts 20:35; 2 Cor 9:6, 11; cf. Prov 14:31; Luke 16:25).

IX. *Exercising Church Discipline*

The only place where we have a glimpse of the Corinthians grappling with the issue of church discipline is when they dealt with the "offender" (2 Cor 2:5–11). The precise nature of the "wrong" involved (2 Cor 7:12) is unknown, but it may have been an insult of some description directed against Paul (see 2 Cor 2:10) or one of his representatives, either by a visitor to Corinth or by some Corinthian who perhaps headed up the opposition to Paul at Corinth and objected to Paul's disciplinary methods such as those outlined in 1 Cor 5:4–5. In this present case, a majority of the Corinthians had evidently followed Paul's instruction and had inflicted some unspecified punishment on "the one who did the wrong" (2 Cor 7:12). Paul now advises, "The punishment inflicted by the majority is sufficient for this person. So now instead, you should forgive and console him, to avoid his being perhaps overcome by excessive sorrow. This is why I urge you to reaffirm your love for him" (2 Cor 2:6–8).

From this whole episode we can identify six stages in successful church discipline.

(1) Wrongdoing, which implies an offending party and sometimes an offended party (2 Cor 7:12).

(2) Punishment (2:6), which is inflicted by "the majority" (2:6).

(3) Pain or sorrow (2:5, 7), which is suffered by the wrongdoer (2:7), and, in a different sense, by the congregation (2:5).

(4) Repentance (implied in 2:6), which is the outcome of godly sorrow (2:10).

(5) Forgiveness (2:7, 10), which is granted by the congregation as well as by "the person wronged/the injured party" (2:12).

(6) Affirmation (2:8), involving restoration to full fellowship within the congregation.

For offences serious enough to warrant corporate church discipline, stages (2) to (5) are not only necessary but must occur in that fixed order. That is, it is inappropriate to move directly from identifying the wrongdoing to offering forgiveness. Repentance must precede forgiveness (see Luke 17:3). The aim of the punishment and pain is not retribution or vengeance but repentance.

It is a grim reality that in this modern age church leaders need to be aware of the possible legal and civil implications or complications that might arise from exercising church discipline of any sort. Certainly, competent legal advice, preferably from Christian lawyers, should be sought and followed before pursuing any type of remedial discipline.

X. *Pastoral Adaptability*

Books have been written about Paul's exemplary pastoral techniques, especially as seen in the Corinthian correspondence and elsewhere, techniques such as his appeal to the example of Christ (e.g., 2 Cor 8:9) or established Christian tradition (1 Cor 11:16); or his secure grounding of his commands or advice on theological facts, with imperatives based of indicatives, "you are; therefore be!" Here the exclusive focus will be on the prime example of his *pastoral adaptability*, namely, his temporary foray into "foolish boasting."

Paul's principal adversaries at Corinth, probably intruders for Judea engaged on a Judaizing mission, had gained a foothold among the believers there by their forthright self-commendation (2 Cor 10:12, 18) as legitimate servants of Christ (2 Cor 11:23) and their callous domineering behavior (2 Cor 11:20). Given their aggressive and persistent boasting (2 Cor 10:12–18; 11:12, 18) and the naïve responsiveness of the Corinthians, the apostle could not avoid a difficult choice—to boast or not to boast. He was doubtless aware of the two juxtaposed proverbs in Prov 26:4–5:

> Do not answer a fool in terms of his folly,
> lest you become like him yourself.
> Answer a fool in terms of his folly,
> lest he imagines himself to be wise.

For Paul to refrain from comparable boasting would appear to validate the false claims and teaching of his adversaries whom he regarded as Satan's minions (2 Cor 11:15). But to engage in foolish boasting in order to regain fully his converts' support might appear to be using worldly tactics (2 Cor 11:18) and underhand techniques (2 Cor 4:2). The former risk was much greater than the latter, so Paul opted to indulge in "a little bit of foolishness" (2 Cor 11:1), which in the event amounted to a substantial quota of foolishness (2 Cor 11:1—12:13)! He indicates his reluctance and embarrassment in adopting his rivals' strategy (2 Cor 11:16, 21b, 23; 12:1, 6, 11) and appeals for the Corinthians' understanding and tolerance (2 Cor 11:1, 16; 12;1), insisting that they had forced his hand (2 Cor 12:11). But he finds compensation and consolation by boasting of his "weaknesses," his sufferings and humiliations (2 Cor 11:23–27, 30–33; 12:5, 9–10), and by boasting "in the Lord" (1 Cor 1:31; 2 Cor 10:17), that is, about who Christ is and what he has done (see Jer 9:23–24).

The minister, pastor, priest or church leader of the twenty-first century may on occasion have to imitate Paul's pastoral adaptability by courageously choosing the lesser of two evils when confronted by an unavoidable choice.